Praise for *Good Money Revolution*

"Inspiring. Challenging. Groundbreaking. *Good Money Revolution* is ready to change your mindset about money." —**Andy Andrews**, *New York Times* bestselling author and founder of WisdomHarbour.com

"You shouldn't have to choose between growing a successful business and impacting the world. In *Good Money Revolution*, Derrick shares how to do both. For business leaders who desire a life of significance, this book is a great guide." —**Michael Hyatt**, *New York Times* bestselling author

"If you want to impact the lives of others by making a difference in the marketplace, you are really going to enjoy this book." —**Bob Goff**, author of *New York Times* bestsellers *Love Does*; *Everybody, Always*; and *Dream Big*

"Generosity is a powerful and underestimated tool of transformation. It changes the world one life at a time, beginning with the individual providing it. *Good Money Revolution* shows you exactly how—and it's worth re-reading again and again." —**John O'Leary**, #1 national bestselling author of *On Fire*

"Derrick Kinney has created the go-to guide on making, saving, investing, and giving more money. Packed with humorous anecdotes and sobering wisdom, I felt like I was reading a treasure map to reach financial freedom while impacting the world. This is a must-read." —**Lara Casey**, CEO of Cultivate What Matters

"Both prosperity and generosity go hand in hand, and Derrick helps you to create more of both in this practical, life-changing book. The time is now for you to join the Good Money Revolution. You can thank me later!" —**Chris Harder**, investor and philanthropist

"We've needed a fresh voice about money for a long time—and Derrick Kinney is that voice. This book should be required reading for every business leader wanting to do more with their money and their life." —**Dr. Nido Qubein**, president, High Point University

"Derrick has cracked the code. Get ready for an honest, hopeful, actionable approach to your money. Derrick's message is exactly what you need right now and it's impossible to read this and not get motivated about your finances." —**Jon Acuff**, *New York Times* bestselling author of *Soundtracks*

"No matter where you're at with your money, Derrick's seven-step Good Money Framework will transform you from an insecure investor to a confident wealth creator. This book will redefine financial planning for decades to come." —**Dr. Brad Klontz**, financial psychologist and author

"If you want to make more money and live the life you've always wanted, Derrick Kinney shares his proven formula to achieve both. This is the book you need right now." —**Dan Miller**, author of *48 Days to the Work You Love*

"Derrick's practical yet powerful strategies and stories will allow you to completely rewrite your money story and create lasting impact in ways you didn't know—until now. Derrick's message is exactly what we need today." —**Barbara Huson**, author of *Rewire for Wealth* and *Overcoming Underearning*

"In a new and insightful way, Derrick tackles the challenging money issues in today's modern economy that most experts shy away from. Derrick reveals the real secret that few business leaders understand: How generosity can boost your bottom line!" —**JV Crum III**, podcast host, coach, founder of ConsciousMillionaire.com

"If you have always believed that money was complicated, confusing, and out of reach, this is the guide you've been looking for. Derrick masterfully demystifies the world of investing with simple, easy strategies you can implement today." —**Justin Donald**, bestselling author of *The Lifestyle Investor*

"What if there was a better way to think about your money? *Good Money Revolution* puts the status quo on notice. A new day for you and your money has arrived." —**Steven Pressfield**, bestselling author of *The War of Art*

"In this persuasive book, Derrick Kinney speaks with the compelling voice of personal experience as he elevates money from the bank account and the complicated economy into a life-transforming medium and metric. I confidently predict it will uplift both lives and fortunes. It provides reasons and explanations that will motivate and inspire readers on their journey through the portal of prosperity." —**Rabbi Daniel Lapin**, bestselling author of *Thou Shall Prosper*

"Derrick Kinney is one of those standout financial authors that simplifies money in a way that flat-out makes sense. You'll love how easy—and fun—this book is to read!" —**Bob Beaudine**, CEO, bestselling author of *The Power of Who* and *2 Chairs*

"Thanks to its lovely colloquial style, reading *Good Money Revolution* feels like a chat with a master storyteller, yet its financial wisdom will transform your life." —**Bea Boccalandro**, author of *Do Good at Work: How Simple Acts of Social Purpose Drive Success and Wellbeing*

"If you're twenty-five and paying off college debt, read this book. If you're forty and teaching your kids about money, read this book. If you're sixty and feel behind on retirement, read this book. Get the message? Read this book." —**Peter Shankman**, author of *Faster Than Normal*

GOOD

HOW TO MAKE MORE MONEY

MONEY

TO DO MORE GOOD

REVOLUTION

DERRICK KINNEY

FOREWORD BY DONALD MILLER

Skyhorse Publishing

Skyhorse Publishing books may be purchased in bulk at special discounts for sales promotion, corporate gifts, fund-raising, or educational purposes. Special editions can also be created to specifications. For details, contact the Special Sales Department, Skyhorse Publishing, 307 West 36th Street, 11th Floor, New York, NY 10018 or info@skyhorsepublishing.com.

Skyhorse® and Skyhorse Publishing® are registered trademarks of Skyhorse Publishing, Inc.®, a Delaware corporation.

Visit our website at www.skyhorsepublishing.com.

10 9 8 7 6 5 4 3 2 1

Library of Congress Cataloging-in-Publication Data is available on file.

Cover design by Matt Lehman

Print ISBN: 978-1-5107-7291-5
Ebook ISBN: 978-1-5107-7292-2

Printed in the United States of America

for
KARA, LAUREN, HANNAH, CONNER, AND DILLON
You are my greatest joy.

To anyone who's ever felt
they're not smart enough, good enough,
or talented enough to make more money
and have an impact on the world.
This book is for you.

Contents

Part 2: Bad Money

Part 3: Good Money Giveaway

Foreword

I REMEMBER STANDING in line with my mother and grandmother outside a church where the government was giving away blocks of cheese to families who qualified for assistance. As I stood in line, I carefully inspected the other kids in line, hoping they didn't go to my elementary school. I didn't want people to know how poor we were. I was embarrassed and, if I'm honest, a little ashamed. Many of my friends were wealthy. At least to me, they were wealthy. Their parents had two cars. They had a garage. Their house had stairs and a second floor with an extra bedroom for guests. These things, to me, were great luxuries.

My mother worked hard. She was a secretary at an oil refinery. She'd dropped out of college to marry my father, who dropped out of the marriage a few years later—not long after I was born. My mother was frugal with money. She subscribed to a newsletter that taught her how to save money. Instead of buying paper towels, we saved the extra napkins we got when we bought fast food. We used powdered milk instead of real milk because it was half the price.

If you were to pause my story right there, right when I was in junior high adding powdered milk to my cereal, you'd likely fill in the rest of the story revealing how I grew up to become poor myself, how I didn't go to college and got a job digging ditches and started drinking and got a woman pregnant and so on and so on.

But the truth is, that didn't happen to me. At fifty years old, I now run a company and consult with other companies about how they can optimize their marketing efforts to increase their revenue. Every month I invest in the stock market. I've taken a percentage of my income and invested in real estate. I've been smart with money, and I've been rewarded for stewarding the money well.

But why? Why did things work out for me financially when my history says they shouldn't have?

I think there was one foundational reason that set me up for success. The reason is this: I was never taught money was bad.

Not once.

My mother did not believe money was wrong or that wealthy people were bad. In fact, right about the time I graduated from high school, my mother went back and finished her bachelor's degree and then continued to earn her master's in business. At sixty years old she completed her education and started a new career running the books for a high-end interior design firm. When she passed away at seventy-two she was rising in a second career. She had our tiny house completely remodeled and bought herself a new car. She regularly took vacations and would call me from interesting places all over America. She loved her life.

It would have been easy for my mother to have felt like a victim in life and painted those with higher means as the villains. She could have taught us that wealthy people make their money off the backs of the poor and that we should beware of them and never trust them.

My mother could have been envious of the wealthy and, in insecurity, resisted ever learning from them.

Instead, she was determined to learn what the wealthy knew about money. And she let me know I could learn from them too.

That single mindset—the mindset that making money is really about knowledge and that any of us could learn how to do it and, more importantly, how to steward it after we got it—is the difference, I believe, between many of the haves and have-nots in this world.

Certainly many people have a greater struggle to get ahead than others, but the solution to those struggles is twofold: opportunity and knowledge. Without opportunity, knowledge is worthless, and without knowledge, opportunity will only lead to failure.

But believing money is a bad tool used by bad people is a nonstarter. Nothing in our society will improve if this becomes the collective belief.

If there's a book I wish my mother had had when we were young, it's this book. Derrick Kinney, in many ways, has written an antidote to personal poverty. He not only teaches us that money is good but also helps us understand what to do with that money.

Read this book carefully, especially if you're somebody who has a good heart. More people with good hearts should have money because good people do good things with money. Hand this book to your kids as soon as they are old enough to read it and let them know they have an opportunity to become wealthy if they so desire. Let them know that money doesn't make you evil but, in fact, can greatly multiply your power to do good.

Money can either be good or bad. Money can be leveraged to hurt or to heal. It all depends on what we do with it. This book will help you increase the amount of good money in the world, and, to me, this should be a mandate for every American. Make good money and do good things with it.

Donald Miller, Business Made Simple
Nashville, Tennessee

From Success to Significance

I WAS NOT destined for success, believe me. A few months ago, my mom gave me a few photographs from my childhood. The first one I looked at was of me in an oxygen tent. Breathing difficulties resulted in frequent trips to the hospital. It's almost hard to remember those years, as if I'm looking at someone else. But no, it was definitely me.

In another picture, I just looked sickly. It reminded me that in elementary school, most days I stayed inside during school recess because of my asthma. I also had a hard time making friends because my dad's work situation forced my family and me to move six times before I even entered the sixth grade. The struggle of always being the new kid was exacerbated by the fact that big noses ran in my family, and I received the full package. As you can imagine, in junior high school I was teased—a lot. As I entered high school, I was trying to find my way, coping with feelings of loneliness, and wondering where I fit in.

My life didn't exactly change overnight, but almost. One day my mom gave me a book called *Go For It!* by Judy Zerafa, which has since become a classic guide to surviving middle school and beyond. There's actually a chapter in it called "How to Be Popular." I read and reread and read it again. One thing led to another, and during my sophomore year in high school, I decided to run for junior class president. I was a nobody—but a nobody with a bold plan. I created a strategy for my campaign posters that went against the grain. Instead of big, bold letters, I put my campaign promises, and even my name, in super small letters that forced people to closely examine what was written. I figured it would be the opposite of what everyone else did and would really stand out.

Election day arrived, and at the end of the day, I anxiously awaited the sound of the intercom crackle. The principal's voice came on and announced the results by grade. "The junior class president is . . . Derrick Kinney!" My friends were clapping. It was a big win for the little guy. I was euphoric. Then suddenly the principal corrected himself. "Junior class president is Melanie Johnson; Derrick Kinney is vice president." I'm pretty sure my jaw dropped. I could not believe it. To say Mr. Griffin's correction was a letdown is a gross understatement. I was disappointed and embarrassed. I came in second, but it felt like a hollow victory.

The following year, with my now vast political experience, I set my sights on being elected student congress president. This was the big one. The odds were stacked against me. My cold, harsh reality was that I did not come from the gene pool of the popular kids. I was a nobody with the heart of a somebody. And I had another bold plan. I knew exactly how I planned to run my campaign. It occurred to me that there were many different groups in our high school—the rock-and-roll crowd, the country-western crowd, the athletes, the band kids—and every day they would hang out in their own preferred spots around the school. I decided to take a photograph of me shaking hands with the leader of each group. Those pictures were going on posters with phrases like "Let's Rock! Vote for Derrick" (for the rock-and-roll crowd) and "Win with Derrick" (for the athletes) in big letters. Of course, the posters were strategically hung where each clique congregated.

My campaign strategy seemed to be gaining traction, and because of that I was learning some key lessons. I had taken the focus off me and put it on others. By making others feel important and allowing them—all those students who also felt like nobodies—to be heard, together we could become somebodies.

It's a powerful moment when a nobody becomes a somebody. Five other people also ran for student congress president, so the stakes were high. At the end of election day, I again anxiously awaited the sound of the intercom crackle. The principal's voice came on. When he announced, "For student congress president, the winner is . . . Derrick Kinney," I waited a minute just to be sure he wouldn't be correcting himself. This time, there was no recanting. I still remember the cheering from my fellow students. It wasn't just me who won that day, it was all of us. Every unpopular kid who was ever told they weren't important or their opinion didn't matter suddenly had a voice and had won the election.

I can still feel the emotions of that day. I realized then and there that you can create your own identity; that if you've been told you can't do something, you're not good enough, smart enough, or talented enough, you, too, have a reset button that allows you to do something new. A fresh start.

Remember that sickly kid who wasn't destined for success? Well, after college (and after taking only one finance class) I went on to build a financial planning business that became one of the most respected in the country. I don't think I could have done that if I hadn't made a bold move in high school and stepped right into the middle of my discomfort zone.

As a financial advisor, I've seen every possible attitude about making money, saving it, spending it, loving it, hating it, and giving it away. While no doubt most people want more money, a surprising number of people, either because of their upbringing or because of their current circumstances, treat money as the enemy. To them, money represents scarcity and strain instead of freedom and opportunity.

In the following pages, I'm going to ask you to make some bold moves. You may have to step right into the middle of your discomfort zone too. You see, I believe money is good and good people should have more of it. Good money in the hands of good people gets good work done.

Here's the truth: The way you're making money right now may leave you feeling empty, no matter the size of your bank account. You keep striving to add another zero to your paycheck, but you're not getting any happier. Money might buy you that nice car, beautiful home, or dinner at a five-star restaurant, but then that wealthy feeling disappears two weeks after you've driven the car off the lot, lived in your home for a while, or digested your wonderful dinner. I've worked with thousands of people during my time as a financial advisor, many of whom started from nothing and made a lot of money so they could live the "rich" life. And yet when we sit in my office together, an underlying dissatisfaction remains. Happiness comes from what you do with your money, not how much you have.

A meaningful life doesn't come from cash or greed. It comes from generosity. Look at yourself in the mirror. If you were gone from this earth, would people remember you because you were wealthy or because of what you did with your life and with your money? How do you want to be respected now and remembered later? It's time to move from success to significance. Here is what's at stake: an unfulfilled and unsatisfied life, with your cash sitting in the bank when it could have made a difference in the world.

A revolution typically starts with a few passionate people who demand change. These outsiders think differently. They know something different is possible. They recognize that the status quo is no longer working, and they wonder why they got stuck in it in the first place. Until you press pause and evaluate how things have always been done, you cannot truly question why you've always done them that way. For too long, money has either been called bad or evil, and people who have it are called both. Some of you have been trapped, thinking that what you're paid right now is your limit and you have little chance of changing it. Or maybe you're making serious dough and enjoying the lifestyle you want, but you've discovered something is missing. You've felt it for a while but couldn't quite put your finger on it. You score positive on finances but negative in fulfillment—and it's time for something more.

These are grounds for a revolution, don't you think? The old way of thinking about money is over. Enough is enough. Your past has passed. Your present is here. This moment, as you're reading these words, is when you can create change—in you and in the world around you. We need you, the Good Money revolutionaries, to stand up and be counted. It's up to us—it's up to you—to march forward and help remake the world. Surely, your goal is not to be the richest person in the cemetery. Many people have made lots of money, but few people will move from success to significance. I want you to be one of them.

Welcome to the Good Money Revolution.

PART 1

Good Money

CHAPTER 1

Money Is Good, So Make More of It

MONEY IS GOOD. I like money, and I'm not ashamed or embarrassed about thinking that way. I enjoy making it, managing it, and giving it away. I love that it has provided a comfortable life for my family and me and that it allows me to help make the world a better place. Money is good because you can use it for good; you can use it to change the world.

I've always believed that money is good. Thinking back to my childhood, I enjoyed it even then—making it, saving it, dreaming of the good I could do with it. Most summers included a two-week visit to my grandparents in Wenatchee, Washington. Sitting on the floor of their living room, I spent hours looking at the Sears, Roebuck and Co. catalog, dreaming of owning the go-cart pictured on page 16. *Wow*, I thought to myself—*if only I had that go-cart, my life would be complete*. I promised myself that someday I would be able to buy it.

I was determined, and I stayed determined long after I had forgotten about the go-cart. Beginning at an early age, I kept a cash book, where I tracked the intake and outflow of every penny that passed through my hands, even the quarter I found on the sidewalk near our home in suburban Arlington, Texas. An amortization chart on the back of my closet door tracked the money I loaned to family and friends. My parents humored me as I loaned

3

them five dollars and charged interest. I had a few entrepreneurial ventures, too, including, at the age of eleven, a bicycle-inspection business. My first client was my nine-year-old sister. I charged her a dollar for a handmade sticker that I attached to her bicycle. She was thrilled.

Growing up, we didn't have a lot of money. My dad was a metallurgical engineer and my mom worked part-time to make ends meet. As a child and into my teenage years, I watched my dad "talk the talk" but struggle to "walk the walk." He would always look for ways to make more money and was intrigued by various opportunities to provide for our family. But he wasn't able to make them sustainable. He got transferred, relocated, and laid off more times than I can count, resulting in six moves before I was in the sixth grade. It took a great toll on me. I felt lonely and frustrated. I never had the newest shoes or clothes or the nice house. In fact, I remember playing my first Little League game in worn blue sneakers from Kmart when everyone else had new, nice white cleats. It was obvious I didn't belong—and I never wanted anyone else to feel that way. Even as a teenager, I was constantly asking myself, *How can I help other people?* My church was sending missionaries to Third World countries and needed money for supplies. The food pantry a few blocks from my house was always in need of more canned goods and volunteers. Everywhere I looked, there were needs waiting to be met.

Once I started working part-time packing grocery store shelves, I began tithing 10 percent to my church and anonymously donating to the local food pantry. (The anonymous part would stick with me.) I knew the number typed on my paycheck wasn't set in stone, that it could grow and be used in bigger ways than I could imagine to help others. Growth and impact were infinite.

It was then that I realized why I liked money. It wasn't for the power or the prestige. Money was a tangible tool that could be used for good, and the more good I wanted to do, the more it motivated me to make more. As a teenager, I intuitively knew what years later I would see confirmed by academic research—that the best thing about making money is the benefit you get by giving it away. When other people had a need, I always asked, "What part could I play in this?" Growing out of that epiphany was a love for investing, saving, and earning.

That year, I started working two jobs—one at Chick-fil-A during the daytime and one at Montgomery Ward selling shoes in the evenings. My hard work caught the attention of my bosses, and they began to open doors for me. I received rewards, raises, and greater responsibility. I knew money was a path to a better way of living. There was something special about coming home from a full day's work and knowing I had added value to my customers' lives. Who doesn't love the bigger paycheck that comes with that? For me, the real magic happened when I gave some of that money to the causes I believed in. It felt like a double return.

Insecurity—the sly beast that rears its ugly head—threatened to return during my junior year in college. I was living at home, working my way through school, but when my dad lost his job due to a mass layoff, he and my mom moved to Oregon, where he had found work. I felt alone. I began to doubt myself. I was on my own and it was a do-or-die moment. I decided that empowerment would replace insecurity. That's when I declared my independence and reminded myself that I could be anyone I wanted to be.

Right out of college, I took a job as a marketing manager for a small software company in Fort Worth, Texas. The company didn't manage their payroll very well and my paycheck bounced twice. Having to tell my church that my tithe check that month was hot was humbling. Another defining moment occurred after our company's product launch, when I was passed over for an expected bonus. I was angry and tired of relying on someone else to tell me how much I was worth. I thought of my dad, who had kept working at jobs he disliked in order to support his family, and I decided I had a choice. I could keep working for someone and rely on them to tell me how much I was worth, or I could take the risk and work for myself. I decided to bet on myself and take the leap. I changed careers and began to pursue my passion of helping people make money. While working full-time, I studied hard, earned multiple licenses, and began building my business, ultimately leaving my job and starting what would become a nationally recognized investment practice.

When I began as a financial advisor twenty-five years ago, I wanted to help people reach the goals that were important to them, and the way to do that was with their money. Money was the tool that could help people enjoy the good life they wanted and do more good for their families, friends, and community. My clients and I were in the same boat, rowing together—as they made more money, I made more.

Then I had another realization. There were many financial advisors for people to work with. Sure, people wanted great returns on their money, and they got them, but they chose me because they felt they were part of something bigger than themselves. I realized that the more I gave back to my local community, the more people wanted to work with me.

Making money just to make money is fun and feels good for a while. But it's like a drug. You need more and more to make yourself feel better—a nicer car, a bigger house, more stuff. You'll find, if you haven't already, that if you want to be truly happy, there has to be more to life than that. There's a saying I love: "Remember when you wished for everything you have now?" Oof. I know. Wherever you are in your life right now, you most likely wished for it at some point. But it's never enough. There will always be another new car to drive, house to build, vacation to take. Money and happiness are not equivalent. Unless you give it away. When you do, you'll often find yourself making more money so that you can give more. It's a motivating cycle. It's the cycle of giving.

The key to your success and having a daily passion that fuels you is to connect your cash to a cause, your money to a movement, your profits to a purpose.

For years, you've probably been thinking you should be making more money, while at the same time, you've wondered how you can play a part in a cause you believe in. Whether you decide to stay in your job or become your own boss, I'm going to teach you how to make more money so you can feel fulfilled and make an impact on the world. But first, let's talk about how money is good—and why you should have a lot more of it.

CHAPTER 2

Does Money = Happiness?

THINK OF A time when you received a bonus at work, a surprise check in the mail, or a gift card from a friend just because they were thinking of you. Or just think of that feeling whenever you remember it's payday! Cha-ching! How do you feel? Angry, disappointed, sad? Probably not. Instead, you're pumping your fist and feeling happy. But we all know that feeling doesn't last.

It's nice to have money. Having enough to stay current on your bills and a little left over at the end of the month is a good feeling. Anyone with the experience of being able to consistently pay off their debts and then their mortgage on the pathway to becoming debt-free knows that it translates into a powerful feeling of satisfaction. There is a happiness and a tranquility that come along with it. Insulating yourself from the pressure of being overwhelmed by your bills reduces anxiety, and the knowledge that you were the one who made good decisions to make that happen and to protect your family—of course, it makes you happy.

Money also has other benefits—like healthy eating. Of course, being able to afford good healthcare and more nutritious foods contribute to your health, but even more than this: money makes you happy and being happy makes you healthy. A study of more than seven thousand adults backs that up. Those who experienced positive well-being were significantly more likely to consume fresh fruits and vegetables and be physically active.[1] Don't prove the old saying to be true that people spend their health chasing wealth, then spend their wealth chasing their health.[2] Money makes you happy, and happy makes you healthy.

Take it from lottery winners, since they're a unique example of people who skyrocketed to wealth from ground zero. According to a report for the Camelot Group conducted by psychology professor Dr. Richard Tunney, lottery winners enjoy healthier lifestyles and are more likely to abstain from alcohol and to exercise.[3] Not a surprise. Good money promotes good health.

Okay, so money makes you healthier. But how much money do you need to be happy? That's where it gets interesting. Obviously, it's difficult to be truly happy if you live in poverty. If you're constantly hungry or cold, or living in an unsafe neighborhood, or if you have no way of getting out of debt, you'll be hard-pressed to say you're happy. Unfortunately, that's true for millions of people, even here in the United States. But still, most don't live in abject poverty, so what about the rest of us? Well, it's a bit complicated.

Researchers rely on data, not anecdotes, and have concluded that while money does make you happy, it makes you happy only up to a point. Economists call it "income satiation," meaning the point at which more income no longer leads to greater happiness. Studies vary, but generally they pinpoint an annual income of something less than $100,000 as the satiation point.[4] Intuitively, this may not seem to make much sense. Even in your almost-six-figure nine-to-five job, can you really be as happy as Jeff Bezos? Maybe you can. Let's explore further.

A few years ago, researchers at Princeton University asked more than 450,000 adults about both their annual income and how often during the previous day they had experienced positive emotions. The researchers defined positive emotions as how much happiness and enjoyment those surveyed had experienced and how much they had smiled and laughed. The Princeton study found that an income between $60,000 to $75,000 was associated with feeling happier than if you made less than that, but after an annual income of about $75,000, there was no relationship between income and happiness.[5]

That's right. Once a person earns about $75,000 a year, more than that is not associated with greater happiness. Other studies have produced similar results.

So if you have a loving family, if you enjoy your job, and if you have friends you can rely on, maybe you really are as happy as Jeff Bezos!

Here's the reality though. Many people get stuck in this cycle of more money equals more happiness. So they work and work and work to build up their bank account, only to look up one day and realize they've done nothing with their money. Just success, with no significance.

You may think that just *having money* gives you meaning. It doesn't. *Giving* is what makes life meaningful; it's what leads to *better* living. We're talking revolution here, because it's time to do something new and different, to live a different kind of life. Think of it as a circular continuum: Earn More → Save More → Give More.

So why doesn't money exactly equal happiness? Let's find out.

CHAPTER 3

What Is Happiness?
Ask Lottery Winners

HAPPINESS IS A difficult emotion to define, so not surprisingly, different researchers use different criteria. Most assess happiness by simply asking people to rate it on a single scale, like one to ten or one to five. Others use what's known as a Satisfaction with Life measurement that tries to determine if a person's living conditions have reached an ideal state and whether, if given the chance, they would change anything important about their life.[1]

But come on, really? You know whether or not you're happy, and you know what makes you happy. And admit it: money is one of the factors that does, no doubt about it. But it certainly isn't the only one.

So what else makes you happy besides the size of your bank account? It turns out that what you do with your money has much more to do with how happy you are than your actual wealth. There's a lot of evidence of this, both anecdotally and through research data. The universe of lottery winners provides proof on both fronts.

I can tell you from personal experience as an investment advisor that stories about lottery winners going broke are not just the work of good fiction writers. I've had clients who, no matter how much conservative financial advice I gave them and regardless of how strongly I told it to them, depleted their winnings because they failed to understand that they'd won a large sum of money, not a printing press. Family and friends come out of the woodwork with their hands out, and the lottery winners can't say no to any of them. Or the winners buy a Porsche or a motorboat they don't need or even use. Or suddenly they think they're the shrewdest investors this side of Warren Buffett. And this is not just anecdotal from my own experience. According to research published in *The Review of Economics and Statistics*, lottery winners who win big are more likely to file for bankruptcy three to five years after winning than those who win smaller cash prizes.[2]

Hold on a minute; I'm about to contradict myself.

Sure, I've known lottery winners who have made spending and investing mistakes, but there is a serious flaw in thinking that both statistical studies and stories about woe-is-me lottery winners support the notion that money is bad, that if you get it, you're going to blow it. Nonsense. Most lottery winners who have come to me for investment advice have made wise decisions and been generous with their newly found cash and are leading happy lives. They certainly did not blow it.

A closer look at academic research tells a similar story. For example, the sample sizes used in the aforementioned study were ridiculously small. The study found that after winning the Florida lottery, forty-seven of those who had won between $50,000 to $100,000, or slightly more than 4 percent, filed for bankruptcy three to five years after their win, and only five (3.4 percent) of those who won between $100,000 to $150,000 went bankrupt in that same timeframe.[3] What about those who won millions? I bet they're pretty darn happy.

Winning the lottery makes you happy. Duh! And it doesn't make you go bankrupt, despite what you read in the media. Although several news outlets have cited a statistic by the National Endowment for Financial Education (NEFE) stating that 70 percent of lottery winners end up bankrupt within a few years after receiving a large financial windfall, this has been discredited. In fact, the NEFE released a statement negating their research as the source of the statistic.[4]

Other studies bear out the obvious: winning a pile of money will put a smile on anyone's face. Yes, a small percentage of lottery winners screw it up and lose it all, but for most, the money leads to positive, long-term satisfaction. That's the unequivocal conclusion of multiple studies, including one published by the National Bureau of Economic Research, which found that for the decade large-prize winners were studied, they experienced "sustained increases in overall life satisfaction."[5]

Imagine if you won the lottery. Overnight you would go from Main Street to Easy Street with not a care in the world. The luxurious house, the sportscar, unlimited vacations—all yours. Sounds great, doesn't it? And then there are the details, and not what you'd expect. Let me explain by contrasting two people for you.

Denise won $2 million in the lottery. She was referred to me by a trusted CPA. Right now, you're probably thinking about all you could do with $2 million. That's a lot of money, right? With a lump sum like this, Denise and I discussed several strategies to generate conservative income so she wouldn't run out of money. I shared with her how, when people receive large sums of money, family and friends come knocking, and it can be hard to say no. So make me the bad guy, I told her. She liked that because it gave her some breathing room. I suggested that she just say that in working with her financial advisor, he had invested the winnings for her long-term retirement.

What happened next is unlike anything I've ever experienced. Something shifted and Denise couldn't say no to anyone. She began to dole out money, and fast. First, she was supporting her grown children and a few grandchildren. Then she bought a bigger house and vacations for her entire family to help create lasting memories. After three months, we visited in my office to review her situation. She had spent $500,000. We had a candid conversation about her goals and the impact her spending was having. We practiced conversations to help her say no to family and friends. When she left the office, she said she felt encouraged and empowered. At least until my phone rang a week later. Her son knew a guy who had an amazing business idea and needed $250,000 to help get it started. I asked her what she knew about the man. She offered only sketchy details and bluntly told me, "Look, it's my son's friend; I think it will be fine. Plus, he's promised to pay me back at 10 percent interest." Reminding her again that my role was to help protect and defend her money, I warned her not to loan a stranger such an immense sum. She politely thanked me and gave me the wiring instructions. This was followed by extravagant birthday gifts for family members because she didn't want to be seen as cheap. She was acting how she thought people expected her to act with so much money. Within two years, she had run through all her winnings and more. Funny thing is, her investments with me had earned quite a bit of money, but not enough to overcome the huge withdrawals she made.

At about this same time, another client, Charlotte, won $3 million. In our conversations together, I encouraged her to use this money as a tool for now, but also for the future. If she could live off a comfortable income, her portfolio would provide for her, and possibly grow to a larger amount. She splurged on a couple items, but diligently stuck to the plan I laid out for her. Her passion was supporting a local nonprofit that provided needy children with Christmas presents. Throughout the year, as parts of the account grew, we would reposition profits to a conservative account, in essence letting the stock market pay for the gifts and making sure the money would be there when needed. Over time, it provided for her, for gifts for a growing number of needy children, *and* grew in value. My philosophy has always been that you want to have something to show for the gains you've made from investing.

Two ladies. Two vastly different stories. One woman wanted to be all things to all people and ran out of money. Another woman was true to herself and generous to the causes she believed in, while at the same time growing her savings further. Similar opportunities. Opposite outcomes.

The message of these stories is not only to be careful with your money, it's that money won't change you. You are who you are. I like the way John O'Leary puts it. John is the author of both *On Fire: The 7 Choices to Ignite a Radically Inspired Life* and *In Awe: Rediscover Your Childlike Wonder to Unleash Inspiration, Meaning, and Joy.* He told me, "Money just makes us more of who we already are. . . . If you decide to be generous when you have little, watch what happens as you grow into wealth. It will make you even more expansive, it'll make you more generous, it'll make you more interesting but also more impactful in the community."[6]

In a way, that's self-evident. Think about your own life. How you spend your money is more important than how much money you have. Of course, you feel happy when you get a raise, or even after finding a five-dollar bill on the sidewalk. But these feelings are fleeting. If you spend your lottery winnings only on yachts and material pleasures, in the end the windfall is going to make you miserable. But if you're prudent, and generous, money is good and more money is better.

CHAPTER 4

Happiness Is What You Do, Not What You Have

I F YOU REALLY want to be happy, use your money for something good.

Be generous. Harvard Business School Professor Michael Norton, coauthor of *Happy Money: The Science of Happier Spending*, has conducted many interesting studies to explore the relationship between money and happiness. For one study, he and his colleagues at the University of British Columbia approached students on campus and gave them an envelope of cash, containing either a five- or twenty-dollar bill, along with a note. For half of the students, the note instructed them to spend the enclosed money on themselves by 5:00 p.m. that day. Every other student was instructed to spend the money on someone else in that same time. Consequently, half the students bought themselves something like a pair of earrings or an ice cream, and the other half spent the money on things like a stuffed animal for a niece or a contribution to a local soup kitchen.

The results were astounding. When questioned later that day, the students who had spent the money on someone else were happier, measured against their baseline from their original interview, than those who spent the cash on themselves.[1]

Mike Norton's team has conducted similar studies all over the world with similar results. It turns out that if money makes you feel selfish, you're not going to enjoy it. "When you buy stuff for yourself, it doesn't feel like you did anything," he told me. "It's nice—you have a new computer, you have a new something—but you didn't have any real impact on anything; it's just a new thing on your shelf. But when you spend money on other people, it gives you a huge feeling that you've had an impact on somebody else, that you've had an impact in general."[2]

The idea that being generous with your money is the key to happiness is also supported by other entrepreneurs. John O'Leary put it simplest, and perhaps best, when he paraphrased Anne Frank,[3] saying, "I've never met anyone who became poor by being generous."[4]

Spending on other people has a ripple effect. It makes us happier because it's a tangible act that today we know we've helped someone else and made a difference in another person's life. Imagine the delight when the people in the car behind you at the drive-thru are told that their bill has been paid. Or the reaction of a friend when you pick up the check at lunch. In return, you get a smile and a "thanks a lot" and, boom! You can see clearly that you've had a positive impact on their day.

Think of this one other way—emotionally, rather than intellectually—which I think is another way to understand these conclusions. Imagine if every one of your colleagues found twenty dollars on their desk one morning. More than likely, they'd put it in their pocket and go about their day in the same way they would have if they hadn't found the twenty dollars. In this case, the company that fronted the money had, in effect, *lost* money, since the cash hadn't motivated anyone to perform any better at their job and hadn't had any impact at all on their life or anyone else's.

But what if everyone were given twenty dollars and told to spend it on a colleague? If the corporate goal was to improve morale and productivity, the company will have made a solid return on its small investment.

These are all clues to one of this book's most important messages: It's *how* you spend your money, not the size of the pile.

Mike Norton points out that many people typically overestimate the effect more money will have on their happiness. They think money is the "magic cure," and they make all their decisions based on whether it will get them more, like their choice of employment. At the same time, they ignore decisions that ultimately pay off in happiness, like how much time they spend with their friends and family.[5]

Money *can* buy happiness, but we need to stop thinking that it has something to do with the amount we accumulate, and instead start thinking about what we're *doing* with the money that truly makes us happy.

An added bonus is that happiness begets happiness. Bestselling author Jon Gordon explained that, according to researchers at Duke University, people who believe in a brighter and better future will take the actions necessary to create it. "We know that optimists work harder, get paid more, and are more likely to succeed in business, in sports," and in every aspect of their lives, he said. "It becomes a self-fulfilling prophecy."[6]

This is such a good clue to how to have a life well-lived. It seems so simple. Start early, start small, but start where you are.

When my kids were younger, I gave them each five dollars. Their eyes lit up. They were already envisioning the candy or toy they would buy. But then I told them it wasn't for them. Their assignment was to think of a cause they would like to donate it to or a friend whose family was having a hard time making ends meet. I explained to them what that meant. After twenty-four hours to think about it, we met again at the kitchen table to hear their plans. One gave it to a family in need, another to our church, and the other two combined their money and gave it to a homeless shelter. Each one of them admitted that at first, they were disappointed the money wasn't for them, but in the end they felt good inside for what they did with it.

Think of the amount of money you have in your bank account right now. Now, after you have that number in your head, I want you to remember something: The number doesn't matter. It's what you do with it that matters—*connect your cash to a cause, your money to a movement, your profits to a purpose.* This is what changes everything.

CHAPTER 5

Generosity Makes You Wealthy

A FEW YEARS ago, Dave, an owner of a local manufacturing company, came into my office. He was a long-time client and whenever we'd meet, I always enjoyed his positive, enthusiastic attitude. But that afternoon I could tell by his body language something was off. "Tell me what's going on," I said.

Dave responded, "Derrick, the business is going great, but I'm no longer into it. I've lost my motivation. I don't really feel a lot of satisfaction."

As we were talking, a thought occurred to me. "Are there any causes or organizations you find interesting and that you would like to support?" I asked him. The question caught Dave by surprise, and he sat back and pondered for a moment. Then he told me that a couple of years ago he and his family had gone overseas and visited a small village with no real school building and no resources to properly educate the children. They had said to themselves, "It'd be neat to do something for these kids," but then they just kind of tucked the idea away, returned home, and went about their lives. "What if you did this?" I suggested. "Over the next twelve months, set a goal to increase your business, and a portion of that increase could go to building that school." His eyes got as big as saucers, and he sat up with a start.

Three months later, Dave returned to my office looking ten years younger, more engaged, with much more zeal for his business and his life. "Derrick," he told me, "you're not going to believe this, but our sales are already up 20 percent, and we've almost fully funded that school." As a business owner, he was reinvigorated. He had found a way to connect profits to purpose. By giving more money, Dave was actually making more money.

This is the untold secret to making more money: giving it away. I call it the "Generosity Purpose." It's the reason my client's life changed—and yours can too.

I want to ask you a question. What injustice do you see that keeps you awake at night? What really bothers you and makes you say, "I want to do something about that"? What wrong do you see in society that you want to make right? Is it in your local community? Is it around the world? What is the cause that you care so deeply about? *Connect your cash to a cause, your money to a movement, your profits to a purpose.* This is what changes everything. This is the Generosity Purpose.

I met with a couple recently who wanted to implement these Good Money principles but weren't sure where to start. Don and Sharla asked, "Derrick, how can we incorporate this into our business?" This particular couple had a recycling company. It had done very well, but they noticed over the past couple of years, not only was their business beginning to drop off, but their excitement and their joy as business owners had also diminished. I asked them what they were passionate about—if there was a wrong they wanted to help make right. They told me so much trash and debris in the oceans really bothered them. They were saddened by the devastating impact it was having on marine life. "We want to help solve that problem," they said. "Maybe not cure the problem, but at least help solve it."

I suggested they reach out to their customer base and tell them, "We've decided to create a Generosity Purpose for our business. A portion of all of our profits will now go toward an organization to help clean the oceans and make them safer for fish and the other animals who live there." As you can imagine, their existing customers were pleased to hear that money they were paying for their recycling services was being used to do more good in the world. Their commitment also allowed them to communicate to potential customers, "We know that you have many options to choose from to do your recycling work, but one of our core values is our Generosity Purpose. A portion of all our profits helps make the world better."

Not only did Don and Sharla's business grow, but they also experienced renewed excitement and joy by connecting a purpose to their profits.

What's your Generosity Purpose? Is it helping abolish sex trafficking? Helping your city's homeless population? Or is it more personal, like funding your children's college tuition or paying for the piano lessons your granddaughter has always wanted to take? It's not about you—but about someone or something that you believe can do more good and leave an impact on the world. After all, the *Me Show* will, one day (I promise), get cancelled. The *We Show* always gets high ratings and airs longer.

Most people lead with, "I want to make more money," but what if you led with, "I want to give more money and to do that, I'll have to *make* more money." This is the path that gives purpose to your money, and to your life—no matter what your job is or your current stage of life. I've seen this light switch flip in many, many of the people with whom I've worked. Here are two examples:

1. Kevin and Michelle, both in their forties, were deeply bothered by the growing homeless population in their

city. They could see the problem but didn't know how to be part of the solution. As we visited together, Michelle shared with me that growing up, her family had very little, and that during a few desperate periods, they had slept in their car and foraged in dumpsters for food. As we talked, I asked what her ideal scenario would be to help the homeless. She wanted to do more than just give the people she saw on the street corners money; she wanted to make a more meaningful impact. She contacted her local shelter about any training programs to help them be self-sustaining and independent. She discovered they were designing a program and needed monthly donors. *This was perfect*, she thought. Fast forward a few months. My heart warmed when she told me she had found her happy place and felt her money was making a real difference.

2. With retirement three years away, Michael and Juanita shared with me a cause they felt passionate about. Now sixty-two, Michael was a devoted pediatrician and they both got a lot of enjoyment from their financial support of an overseas medical organization that provided access to quality medical care to remote villages. For thirty-seven years, Michael had seen firsthand how his patients benefited from quality treatment. He felt it wasn't right that all children didn't have that same benefit. Most recently, they had supported missions that were providing aid in Guatemala and Haiti. Showing me some of the photographs they had received, I could see how much it meant to them. "When I retire, we're going on a mission trip ourselves," he said, smiling. "With each patient I see here in Texas, I know it's helping me make money to help more children around the world."

Each of these individuals discovered the pleasure of finding and implementing their Generosity Purpose.

You might believe that making a lasting impact on the world—or even your small community—requires loads of cash. That's not even a little bit true. Start small. Impact one person at a time. As you do that, you'll realize you are changing *their* world and *the* world.

In the past, you may have given money out of obligation, like to a fundraiser for your child's school or a cancer research fund when you check out at the grocery store. If you're honest with yourself, you sometimes (or frequently!) question why you would give away what you've earned. After all, what's mine is mine, right? Others of you may be intrigued by the idea of giving more, but don't know how to get started.

Here's what I know: You reap what you sow. Regardless of the attitude toward giving that you have now, I'm asking you to rethink money—to rethink its purpose. Imagine a cause you have felt passionate about ever since you were young but didn't think you could do anything about. Now is your chance. Small or big, just get started. This is where the fun begins.

Many entrepreneurs I interviewed for this book emphasized how important it is to start early to become accustomed to both making money and giving it away. That's because both behaviors become muscle memory, as do their corollaries—bad earning and saving habits and an accompanying stinginess.

Rabbi Daniel Lapin, author of *Thou Shall Prosper: Ten Commandments for Making Money*, suggests that when generosity is instilled at a very early age, it generally sticks, and that teaching our children to be givers makes for more successful living. "As soon as you train that muscle, and you learn to unloosen that closed, tightly gripped fist, you are now in a much better position to succeed in business," he told me. "Apart from anything else, you are willing—or more willing, I should say—to do something very important, which is not try and do everything yourself but hire other people to do the things that you're not particularly good at."[1]

As I visited with clients, we would talk about the impact of the economy on their money. But I would point out to them the difference between the overall economy and what I referred to as their personal economy. For example, while knowing the key economic indicators, such as whether unemployment was up or down or the health status of the overall economy, was important, what really mattered was their ability to put food on the table and save for personal financial goals (like saving for their kids' college tuition, having enough money to travel in retirement, and spoiling the grandkids). In other words, what does all this economy stuff mean to *me*? It's easy to think that making a lasting impact on the world, or even your community, requires loads of cash. But that's thinking like the overall economy. I'm suggesting you make it simple; do what you can, where you are right now as an outflow of your personal economy. Start small and simply impact one person at a time. That's how you start to change the world.

I liken this idea to the first time I spoke to an audience of several thousand people. I was terribly nervous. The thought of all those eyeballs staring me down felt ominous and overwhelming. It wasn't one big eyeball staring at me, it was thousands of individual pairs. I pictured myself sitting in the audience watching another speaker on stage. Then I was onstage but speaking just to one person among the thousands in front of me. As I spoke, I focused on just one pair of eyes at a time, trying to help one person at a time—making a difference in their world only. That's what I try to do: build my own wealth one dollar at a time, and give a helping hand to others, one person at a time.

When you start earning and saving with a purpose that excites you, it will motivate you, lighting a fire within you that burns so bright that it will lead to success in every area of your life. It will motivate you to do whatever you have to do to build your bank account—whether it's being successful in your job, getting a raise, starting a side hustle, or growing your own business. You will acknowledge your power to radically revolutionize your family's future and the future of the world around you.

You have two paths you can take. Path 1: Keep making money and stay unhappy and unfulfilled. Path 2: Make good money and lots of it, but do it by adding meaning to your money.

If you choose path 1, you are leaving money and a lasting legacy on the table that could benefit you and your family. You're missing out on helping right the wrongs that bother you the most. It's not enough to say, "I'm going to work now so I'll have more to give away later." It means nothing unless it's attached to a powerful emotion that you will feel when you've made a real impact.

If you choose path 2, you're now ready to start earning with a purpose. After all, if you don't have money, you can't give any away.

I'm asking you to rethink your attitudes about money and giving, and to join the Good Money Revolution. One person at a time, your money can impact the world.

CHAPTER 6

Pairing Purpose with Profits

EVEN BIG CORPORATIONS are beginning to understand that giving is profitable, both because it's the right thing to do, and frankly, because it's good business. Everyone benefits—employees, customers, and the bottom line.

Bea Boccalandro, author of *Do Good at Work: How Simple Acts of Social Purpose Drive Success and Wellbeing*, has spent decades researching the impact doing good has on employees and business. Bea says studies show that "Those who feel their work does some good for the world have increased employee engagement—meaning they put more effort into their work—as well as increased productivity and retention."[1] At the Canadian company Manulife Financial, an internal study discovered that employees who felt like they were helping others as a part of their workweek had 60 percent less turnover than those who didn't.[2] Research even finds that people are more creative and more optimistic if they feel like they're working for something larger than themselves.[3]

Companies ignore this reality at their own risk. Brands that don't take giving seriously can count on their employees being de-motivated. "They'll underperform, they'll be dissatisfied, they'll be disengaged, they'll have higher turnover, and they'll sell less," Bea said. "And, by the way, they'll probably steal some supplies too."[4]

It's well known in the corporate world that consumers feel more positive about their buying experience when they know that at least a part of the purchase price is going to a good cause and is having a positive impact. Sometimes, like with the sock company Bombas, giving is in the form of donating the company's product to those who need it most. For every purchase, Bombas donates an item on the purchaser's behalf. Since its founding in 2013, the company has given away more than fifty million items to over 3,500 community organizations.[5] And that's just one of thousands of examples of corporate America giving back. For other companies, it's everything from lowering their carbon footprint, to supporting health and educational services, to helping veterans reenter the civilian workforce.

Companies find that connecting their products and services to their Generosity Purpose actually enhances their bottom line. Customers and clients will actually pay more to align with a cause they believe in. Imagine an issue you feel passionate about. Wouldn't you be more likely to purchase a product or service from a company that was putting its own dollars toward those same goals?

In a client retention study, one of Bea's clients emailed half of its customer base informing the group of the environmental efforts the company was making. The company used solar panels, had stations available for recharging electric vehicles for employees and customers, and even had its own garden. The study found that compared to the half who did not receive the email, the group made aware of the company's environmental efforts purchased significantly more of that company's product. So much more, in fact, that at first the client questioned the accuracy of the data.

Would you be surprised to know there is also a biological component at work here? According to Bea, researchers found that "if you look at a regular ad, selling you ... a car [for example], and it has nothing to do with any societal cause out there, you respond a certain way, just biologically. If that same ad helps ... the US Olympic team or puppies or Save the Whales or some societal cause, the way we react to that ad, biologically, what happens in our brain cells, is similar to gazing into the eyes of someone we love."[6]

In other words, corporate philanthropy is good business. I take these lessons personally because I believe the dynamic of people wanting to work with people and businesses who give was a major reason for the success I had as an investment advisor. I knew full well that people could invest their hard-earned money with any number of professionals, so I came to realize they chose me for two reasons. First, I seemed to know what I was doing to help them make money and reach their goals, which was made clear by the performance of their investments. And second, and at least as important, quite often they liked feeling part of something bigger than themselves, bigger than just seeing the value of their investments grow. My wife, Kara, and I happen to be passionate about education, so we support our local schools, and a lot of people liked that. I encouraged my clients to get involved in their own communities, and they liked that too. If people felt smart about having an experienced financial advisor helping them manage their money, they felt even smarter if at the same time, they were helping the community where they lived and worked.

Bea sums it up well: "When people perceive you as a giver, they perceive you as someone who cares about the community," she writes. "They're more likely to trust you, and it causes stickier relationships because they don't just work with you; now they

33

work with you and the causes you're a part of, which become a big part of what's important to them."[7]

Listen to me. A person can buy anything—a pair of socks, a new couch, or a new house—from any number of sources, but how will you at the same time make people's lives better? One way to do that, which dramatically worked for my business, is by saying, "Look, I'm either going to support certain local causes with my business, or when you become a client of mine, I will donate a portion of revenue I receive either to a cause you select or one we're both passionate about." Most people want to be part of something bigger than themselves even if it's just buying a pair of socks or a piece of furniture; they want to know that one purchase with their money made a difference in the world.

The beauty of good money is that we're pairing purpose with profits. We're putting meaning into money, and by giving more, you're going to be attracting more people who want to work with you. You're going to make more money, so you can give more money.

Drew Holcomb, with his wife, Ellie, made Drew Holcomb and the Neighbors into one of the country's best-known Americana bands. They have a terrific, unique sound, but they consider themselves much more than a musical group; their music is also a way to spread a message of giving. "I definitely think financial success is a reputable goal in any sort of enterprise," Drew told me. "But it can't be the *only* goal, or else it can be unsatisfying."[8] He also said, "As long as you see money as a tool for creating opportunities for generosity and for fun and for taking care of people, then I think, you know obviously, [financial] success is a good thing."[9]

Often at his concerts, Drew announces a local charity and urges his audience to support it. On stage, he talks about the importance of a giving heart, even crediting that spirit for the success of his band. "I've found, as we've built our team over the years, if we can sort of lead with generosity in the way we pay people or how we take care of people, then typically everybody works harder and the enterprise grows naturally. And the times that I've been the most tight with money is when . . . you get less buy-in from your team."[10]

It pays—literally—to be generous. This is the untold secret to making money—using it to fuel your Generosity Purpose.

You're ready to start earning with purpose, giving to causes you believe in, and living a meaningful life. I want to introduce you to the 7-Step Good Money Framework so you can earn more, save more, and give more than you ever thought possible.

CHAPTER 7

The Good Money Framework

Y OU KNOW THAT feeling you get on Sunday about 4:00 p.m.? The realization sets in that tomorrow is Monday. Your entire mood changes. Weekend mode is over. Worry mode has begun. Let's press the pause button.

Instead of being stuck where you are, I want to offer you something else. It's a little four-letter word called *hope*. In Stephen King's book *Rita Hayworth and Shawshank Redemption*, which inspired the 1994 movie starring Tim Robbins and Morgan Freeman, the character Andy pens a letter that says, "Remember, hope is a good thing, Red, maybe the best of things, and no good thing ever dies."[1] Andy wasn't just talking about a pie-in-the-sky, ethereal mentality that's only meant to tickle your ears. Rather, the hope Andy expressed moved him to a patient plan of action that eventually led to his freedom.

This kind of hope is the real deal. A hope that moves you to take action. I want you to imagine how you would feel if on Sunday at 4:00 p.m. your perspective changed and you were looking forward to going to work the next day because you are now working for a bigger purpose. You are working to help make people's lives better, right a wrong, or solve an injustice.

It's a small but revelatory shift that will launch you into your personal Good Money Revolution.

Wherever you are is where you currently are. I know it sounds like a fortune cookie, but it's true. You are where you are and that's where you start. Taking the focus off your job plight and devoting your attention to giving a portion of what you earn to help make the world around you better is like a cold drink on a hot summer day. It feels good. It injects a newfound motivation.

Let me shoot straight with you. It's still work, and you still need to work. But if you have to work, I'm offering you options: Either stay at your current job or find a new one (I know that's easier said than done). If you stay, begin to find purpose in your work. What is it about your job that is helping you accomplish something bigger than yourself? Becoming more productive will invariably lead you to making more money. Or it will light a fire inside you and you will decide to pursue new opportunities that more closely align with your interests and passions. You see, work is involved in both scenarios, but I want your working to feel like you're winning.

Right now you're probably thinking, "All right, Derrick, that sounds great, but tomorrow is still Monday and I'm not looking forward to it." Put one foot in front of the other, think bigger than yourself, and you'll get there.

Live your life with a level of causation—or we'll call it "cause-action"—because achieving the life you want requires you to take action. This is about you making a conscious decision to determine if you want your life to stand for something. To make a difference. To make your community better. To make the world, or someone's world, better.

This quote hangs on a wall in my garage. It is often attributed to Ralph Waldo Emerson but more likely it evolved from an essay written by Bessie A. Stanley.[2] Regardless of its origins, I read and reflect on it often as it reminds me that by helping improve the lives of others, my life gets better too:

To laugh often and much; to win the respect of intelligent people and the affection of children; to earn the appreciation of honest critics and endure the betrayal of false friends; to appreciate beauty, to find the best in others; to leave the world a bit better, whether by a healthy child, a garden patch, or a redeemed social condition; to know even one life has breathed easier because you have lived. This is to have succeeded.

I know you want to make the world better, but you don't have a plan to get there. You're not alone. Many people I meet don't have a clear picture—not only their money picture, but their life picture. You have so many choices; don't succumb to thinking they're limited. And don't be overwhelmed. Live your life like you own it, not like you're renting it from someone else.

Brian Buffini runs the largest real estate coaching company in America. When he talks, people listen—me included. In a recent speech, he described what he calls the "Moling Principle." It's when a person begins to pursue a goal and they dig, dig, dig, dig, and unknowingly get off track. When they finally pop their head up like a mole, they wonder, "How in the world did I get here?"[3]

Has that ever happened to you? It's not that you're not working hard; it's just that you don't have a plan. Or life happens. You get side-tracked, or a crisis pushes you off-track and suddenly you end up in an unexpected place and you have no idea how you got there. The days go by, then the weeks, which turn into months and years. Then suddenly, you're way off course and wonder to yourself, *What happened?*

Best-selling author and entrepreneur Michael Gerber points out a big difference between saying, "It is my intention that . . ."

and "I hope that . . ." Hope has to do with something outside of what is in your control. Intention has everything to do with your actions. "Intention is an act by our mindset," Gerber told me. "Hope is a wish." *I hope, I hope, I hope, I hope.* "Oh my goodness, stop hoping—let's make it happen," he advised. "Intention is a declaration; the difference is night and day."[4]

Wherever you put your intention, vision, and energy is where doors of opportunity will begin to open. It's time to make a plan for your life and money. This is where the Good Money Framework comes in. It takes all that we've discussed thus far and summarizes it into seven simple steps. These seven steps will provide you with a strategy for setting goals and creating a personalized plan so you can execute them successfully.

Step 1: Discover your Generosity Purpose.

When my daughter Hannah was seven, she loved horses. There is a horse farm that backs up to a park near our house. We would occasionally go to that park with carrots or apple slices to treat the horses. Hannah noticed that one particular horse never wore a bridle. In her seven-year-old mind, this really concerned her. She wanted to buy a halter for that horse. She spent money she had saved and purchased a pink halter for the horse and we took it over to the owner's home with a plate of cookies one sunny spring afternoon.

When I earned my first paycheck as a teenager, I began giving to the local food pantry. That was where my Generosity Purpose began. As newlyweds with tight finances, we always made sure to give to our church. In those days there was often more month than money. If we heard about a need and wanted to do something about it, our only option was to cut a few dollars from another of our budget items. As our income grew, we were able to grow our Generosity Purpose. This past year, we were able to make multiple one-time donations to organizations we believe are doing good work in the world locally and abroad. Each month we sponsor several orphaned children as well as support local people who are impacting our community. Years ago we told a local pastor and friend who travels regularly overseas to let us know when he needs a plane ticket. We've purchased quite a few plane tickets over the years. We frequently have young couples and college students over for dinner or take them to lunch. The point is not to give you an extensive list of our personal giving, but to get your brain thinking. Generosity is not a one-time event or check 2051 out of your checkbook. It's a way of thinking: a Generosity Purpose.

Think back to when you were a child or fast-forward to the present. What is a cause that you care deeply about, a wrong you want to right, an injustice that you see? It may be around the world. It may be within your own local community. No matter where it is, you've always thought it would be nice to do something toward that goal. What are those passions? Is it childhood cancer, a lack of drinking water, homelessness, a family in need, or the college kid who would love a home-cooked meal once a week? The Generosity Purpose is a pathway either to give your time, give your money, or both. Let's decide what yours is.

Now I want you to think about one cause that you would like to begin making a financial contribution toward. Don't worry about the amount right now. Just think about the organization or cause you want to support so when you lay your head on your pillow at night, you know you're making a difference. Then fill in the following blanks.

Exercise—Fill in the blanks:

- When I see [insert name of issue you feel passionate about] not being addressed, I feel [insert emotion that you feel].
- I am passionate about [insert issue you feel passionate about] because [fill in reason why]. If I don't take action now, here's what could happen: [fill in the blank].
- [Fill in the blank] is an organization I trust to help alleviate the issues or concerns I most care about.
- Say to yourself, "I am working today so I can help [issue you feel passionate about]. Today, I am helping/working to make someone's life better."

If not me, if not you, then who? Wake up each morning with a purpose. Write down or read aloud your Generosity Purpose.

Step 2: Determine your top three financial goals.

My client Jimmy wanted to retire. He had definite things he wanted to accomplish. We talked about his financial goals as he neared retirement. He wanted to pay off his house, vacation with his wife twice per year, and make frequent visits to see his daughter and her family (well, we all know it was really to see the grandkids) who had recently moved out of state. For Jimmy, these were his three most important financial goals.

We're not ready to make a comprehensive financial plan just yet, but think about your top three financial goals. Narrowing down the things you want helps you get laser-focused. When you know what you're working toward, you're more likely to achieve it. And if you write them on a sticky note or index card and tape it to your bathroom mirror so you see it every day, studies have shown you are exponentially more likely to achieve those same goals.

Financial planning and money management have been made so complicated. I want to keep it simple. Write your top three financial goals. Maybe it's that you want to retire, or pay down a particular debt, put your kids through college, or experience Disney with your grandkids. Whatever it is, just write it down—one, two, three. Now you have some clarity. We're taking out the binoculars and we're getting focused on what we want to do. That's the way to make progress.

Whatever those goals are, they're all unique to you. By focusing energy on your top three, you'll create quick momentum, see progress faster and, as a bonus, your other less-important goals are often reached because you're focused on the biggest, most important ones.

Exercise—Fill in the blanks:

- **Goal 1:** [name of goal] is important to me because [insert reason]. When I achieve this goal, I will feel [insert emotion]. I will accomplish this goal by [date].
- **Goal 2:** [name of goal] is important to me because [insert reason]. When I achieve this goal, I will feel [insert emotion]. I will accomplish this goal by [date].
- **Goal 3:** [name of goal] is important to me because [insert reason]. When I achieve this goal, I will feel [insert emotion]. I will accomplish this goal by [date].

Step 3: Determine your desired income.

Now, Step 3 may sound like a loaded question. Typically, most people answer "more." But I want you to think about where you are right now. What income would reflect what you feel you are worth? Just write that number down. Don't be pie-in-the-sky crazy, but don't short-change yourself either. And remember what psychologists and researchers tell us. More money makes us happy, but only up to a point, and only if we do something purposeful with the money. Now you have an end game. By making more money, you're able to give more money. It's working in tandem. You're making more money, you're saving more money, you're helping others.

Consider your income right now. Are you barely making ends meet? Is there a little left over and you'd like a much bigger cushion? Or are you and your significant other both working full-time and one of you would like the flexibility to stay at home? While it might be a stretch, is it possible both to increase your income and reduce expenses? Is your goal to earn an extra $250, $500, $1,000, or more per month? I've guided people to earn significantly more than that. Remember, this is based on your unique desires and goals.

Most people talk about wanting to make more money, but they don't actually put the pencil to the paper to determine how much money they truly want. You're going to change that now.

Exercise—Fill in the blanks:

- My desired yearly income is: $ [fill in amount].
- Earning this amount of money is important to me because it will allow me to [insert reason].
- Being able to give to [insert organization] will make me feel [insert emotion].

Step 4: Review your options for earning more money.

Maybe you're stuck in a job where you can't make more money, no matter how productive you are. Your salary falls in a certain pay range, has been capped, or it's based strictly on seniority.

Susan taught first grade at a local elementary school and had been a teacher there for over twenty years. She had won teacher of the year and was one of those teachers every parent wants their child to have. Over the years, teachers began asking for her help managing their classrooms. Someone suggested Susan write a "how-to" on classroom management for new teachers. Susan quickly discovered there was a large demand for the information as sales of her self-published book increased and she became a sought-after speaker at teacher conferences. Now, ask yourself these questions: What am I naturally good at? What do I enjoy doing? What is fun? What are people willing to pay me to do? Is there a need in the marketplace for a service I can provide? Your answers to these questions could be the beginning of your new side-hustle and making more money doing what you enjoy.

I ran into a friend at a fast-food restaurant recently. He said he recently became a DoorDash driver, delivering food on evenings and weekends when he was free. His daughter was newly engaged and in the throes of planning her wedding. I laughed when he told me, "Why should I use my money to pay for her wedding? I'll use other people's money to pay for her wedding." Delivering fast food was funding his daughter's wedding.

If your income potential is currently limited, your options may be to evaluate other higher-paying job opportunities or stay in the job you're in and begin evaluating side hustle options. Maybe it's doing more of what you do in your day job, but for select customers on the side. Or perhaps you have an untapped talent or interest that you could pursue in the evenings and on weekends like tutoring, teaching, coaching, or consulting. Or you could work a part-time job.

If you are in a position where you could earn more money, what should you do? The worst thing to do is demand a raise from your boss and say, "If you don't pay me more money, I'm out of here." Sure, it may yield a short-term pay increase, but I'm here to help you earn a sizable amount of money over the long-term. Instead you want to ask how you can add more value to the company you're at, like helping contribute to the growth of the business and increase sales. Or you may choose to study for an additional certification or learn an additional skill to enhance your value. Write down some ideas, talk with your boss, and let them know you want to contribute more to the company and want to make more money by adding more value.

Remember your Generosity Purpose. Think about how the extra money will positively impact you and your family and make a difference for the causes you feel passionate about.

Exercise—Fill in the blanks:

- I could make more money in my current job by [fill in the blank].
- I could talk to my boss about responsibilities and actions such as [fill in the blank] that could result in a raise.
- I could make money working part-time by [fill in the blank].
- I could make money by creating a side gig, such as [fill in the blank].
- I could make more money if I took additional classes, completed specialized training, or earned a professional designation at [fill in the blank].

Step 5: Create a simple saving and investing plan.

My wife and I recently hosted an engagement party for a young couple in our home. As the night came to an end, the woman asked my wife how we handled our finances when we first got married. She and her fiancé had had several conversations about money but struggled to create a plan for their finances after they married. We decided to set a future dinner date to talk more about it.

Money is complicated. The problem is that it's been over-complicated. I'm not saying there are not any complicated money situations. I've run across quite a few as a financial advisor. Even the most challenging scenarios, when they're broken down into smaller bites and simpler steps, are a lot easier to act on. After twenty-five years of guiding clients in setting and achieving financial goals, I discovered that the simplest plans got implemented. And people achieved results. The more complicated plans gathered dust.

Start with these steps. What's coming in each month? Decide on your priorities. Break it down. For example, your priorities are growing your giving fund, saving for retirement, and paying down debt. So you put 10 percent into your giving fund, save 10 percent toward your retirement, and apply the same amount toward debt. You have a plan. You're locked and loaded; you've eliminated the guesswork. Proactive preparation pays off. (I know, it sounds cheesy. But you'll remember it.)

Exercise—Fill in the blanks:

- I want to save [insert amount] this month in order to meet my top three financial goals. Therefore, I must commit [insert percentage] of my paycheck every month.
- I want to put [insert amount] toward debt I want to pay down. To meet this goal, I must commit [insert percentage] of my paycheck every month.
- I want to give [insert amount] of my paycheck every month to help [insert organization]. To meet this goal, I must commit [insert percentage] of my paycheck every month.

Step 6: Implement your generosity strategy.

You have thought about your Generosity Purpose. You've written it down. Now the key is to start. Keep your generosity money in motion each month to have impact. Don't wait. Look at your list and determine what actions to take. When it comes to giving, the present value of money is worth more than the future value of money. Now mathematically, you may say, "Well, Derrick, that makes no sense. If I put $100 into the account right now and watch it grow, it's going to be worth more down the road." Yes, it will, but if you wait ten years to give it away, that is ten years' worth of impact that was lost because the money wasn't actively engaged. No matter what the amount—$5, $10, $20, $100, or more—that money needs to leave your possession each month so that it can start making the world better right now. It's about making sure your money is in motion—for yourself and for others.

If you're working with a financial advisor, make sure they are aware of your Generosity Purpose and are helping you achieve your giving goals.

Exercise—Fill in the blanks:

- I want to give [insert amount] to [insert organization name].
- To meet this goal, I must commit [insert percentage] of my paycheck every month.
- Is my Generosity Purpose reflected in my savings and investing plan? Y/N
- Is my financial advisor aware of my Generosity Purpose and helping me achieve my giving goals? Y/N

Step 7: Track your wealth-building and generosity progress.

Make tracking fun. Okay, the truth is, I think it is fun. My wife wouldn't exactly call tracking our progress "fun"—but she is coming around.

Each quarter, sit down with your spouse, friend, financial advisor, accountant, whomever it may be. Track not only your progress toward your financial goals but your progress with your Generosity Purpose. Ask yourself a few questions: What is going well? Did anything side-track my goals? Do any changes need to be made in order to better accomplish my financial and generosity goals?

I don't sit down with my kids and share all my financial goals. As they have gotten older, we have more conversations about how we spend money and how we make purchasing decisions. We talk about the importance of not incurring debt and staying within a budget. Though our children do not know total dollar amounts or all that we give money to, since they were young we have included them in the giving discussions. We asked what they were thinking about, what was important to them. Consider sitting down and sharing giving strategies with your children. Is there something that, as a family, you feel passionate about around which you can rally together and support? Share with them updates or benefits others receive from your generosity. When our kids were young, they looked forward to the letters we received from the children we sponsored. Those letters were often accompanied by community updates and needs that were met. We shared that with our children so they knew the practical impact our money was making and the good it was doing.

Exercise:

1. Schedule a time ninety days from now to track progress toward your financial goals and your Generosity Purpose.
2. Set a family meeting to discuss your family's Generosity Purpose that you can work toward together.

Slow steps in the right direction are faster than running without a plan. This is where the Good Money Revolution begins— by connecting your **cash to a cause**, your **money to a movement**, and your **profits to a purpose**.

Regardless of the size of your bank account, giving is easier with an abundance mindset. It all starts with *believing* you have the ability to make more, save more, and give more. Throughout this book, I will give you strategies that connect each step in the framework. Now that you've clarified your Generosity Purpose and your financial goals, let's talk about investing. It can feel complicated, but if you're not doing it, it's probably costing you.

CHAPTER 8

Investing: Buckets and Lanes

START BY UNDERSTANDING that you make money twice. First, you work hard to earn it. Then you must work hard to wisely invest and grow it.

One of the biggest mistakes I see people making is waiting to invest. The power of investing comes from doing it early and often and by taking advantage of earnings and dividends. Compounding on those earnings and dividends, with the opportunity of time, will help you build exponential wealth. It's not even about how much you earn; it's about staying consistent with investing the small amounts you have, as often as you can, over time.

Another mistake people make is not having clear objectives and goals as to why they are investing. Are you investing for retirement, to pay for your child's college, to start your own business in ten years, or to move to a different city? When you're not clear on your goals and you see the stock market going through wild short-term swings and start to panic, you'll invariably start to sell at a loss because you weren't really clear on why you were investing. If it's for the long-term, you know that you can weather a short-term disturbance in the market because you know you don't need this money for another decade or two. You have that in mind. Trying to time the market and expect overnight returns is extremely dangerous.

Even the best traders on Wall Street struggle to predict what the market will do tomorrow. When things get hard, go back to your why. Everyone's why is going to be different, and also keep in mind that your why can evolve. When I first graduated college and started earning my first paycheck, my big why was to get on my feet financially. Then it became providing for my family and paying for my kids' college. Now it's growing my business and achieving financial independence.

Standard investment advice includes emphasizing the importance of not having all your eggs in one basket. That's good advice, whether you're talking about investing in another's success and happiness, or more traditional investments using your own money. In the latter case, you shouldn't have more than a certain amount in stocks, bonds, mutual funds, or real estate. Diversify! That way, when one type of investment goes down, another is hopefully going up.

I believe there are three buckets of investing.

Bucket #1: Invest for yourself. Making money is fun. As a business owner, I love that feeling when I create and add value to people's lives so they can make money and I, in turn, make money myself because it's a win-win. When you think of money like a game, it helps simplify things. Money chases value. Add value to people and their money will chase you.

Working hard for your money isn't enough, however. Leaving your money to hang out in your checking account won't cut it. Your money deserves better treatment. It's ready and willing to work for you, so put it in places where it will.

Bucket #2: Invest in yourself. The colors and sounds of fireworks are memorable for me. They shoot up in the air, brilliantly light up the night sky, then fizzle out. Has that ever happened to you?

You're highly motivated for an important project. You give it your all, but it ends up taking everything out of you. Then you're burned out. Or there's the man I spoke with recently who told me that instead of gaining twenty years of experience in his job, he had simply repeated one year, twenty times. He had progressed neither professionally nor personally. Reading a book once a month on what you're good at to get better is investing in yourself. Take a weekend away to refocus. Ask yourself what's important to you and whether you are moving closer or drifting further away from it. As I'll explain shortly, it was a powerful time away like this that led me to sell my business and pursue my passion.

Bucket #3: Invest in others. If you want me to get emotional, invest in my children. When I see a friend, a coach, or a teacher encourage or motivate my children, it pulls hard on my heartstrings, and I may or may not have a tear roll down my cheek. I've come to realize why. It's because I absolutely love investing in others and helping extract every ounce of potential a person has. I've also come to understand the power of the two-ears principle: What you say to your kids often goes in one ear and out the other. What you say to someone else's kids often goes in one ear and stays there. Seeing the impact a small act of kindness or encouragement has on another person is one of the most rewarding experiences you can have. Every Tuesday evening Kara and I host what we call family dinner at our home. Young couples gather around our table while we provide the food. It's a safe place where they can be themselves and we get to be part of their lives. They are some of our greatest and most valuable investments.

Go back with me to the concept of your money working for you. One way to make certain your money is working for you properly is to think of your investment strategy as four lanes on a superhighway.

When you are driving down the highway in your white Honda Accord or fire-engine-red Ferrari (you get to choose) and you see the lane next to you start moving faster, what do you do? You quickly move out of the slow lane you are in. Then what happens? The lane you just moved out of starts moving ahead, and you think you should have stayed where you were. The solution is to have a car in each of the four lanes. Now you have all strategies covered.

Lane #1: Checking or savings. Imagine you're driving in the far right-hand lane, which is typically the slow lane. That's going to be your checking or savings account. That money isn't accumulating much interest, but it's safe, nicely tucked away, and easily accessible through an ATM. It's not going to earn very much, maybe $\frac{1}{10}$ of 1 percent these days, so it's definitely not your get-rich-quick fund.

Lane #2: Two-to-five-year lane. What does that mean? Well, let's say you're saving for a house or a nice family vacation, but at the same time you want to pay off a certain amount of debt. This lane of your investments is not as conservative as a checking or savings account. Maybe it's earning 3–4 percent interest. These are your high-quality investments, so they're not going to be tremendously volatile if the market suddenly drops. The worst thing you can do is use this lane for high risk, aggressive investments and find that when you need the money, it's not there. That would be a huge disappointment.

Lane #3: Retirement lane. Now let's take a look at the next lane over, the second lane from the left. This is the long and steady part of your portfolio—think well-established, blue chip, dividend-paying investments, like stocks, real estate investment trusts, exchange traded funds, mutual funds, annuities, and bonds. While these may fluctuate with the market, they offer growth potential and are part of a well-diversified portfolio. Keeping in mind your risk tolerance and investment time frame, this is the lane for retirement accounts such as 401(k)s, 403(b)s, and IRAs.

Lane #4: Play account. Finally, move over to the far-left lane, the fastest lane on the highway where you're most likely to get a speeding ticket. Let's call this lane your play account. Maybe you heard about an investment a friend or coworker made a ton of profit on and you missed out. This is the kind of investment you might want to put a little bit from your portfolio into to take advantage of a hot stock or a speculative investment. These can be risky, but the bulk of your money is diversified among the other three lanes. Driving in all four lanes will allow you to earn money twice. First, you work hard to earn it and second, you invest it wisely.

"Save like a pessimist, invest like an optimist," says Morgan Housel, a former columnist at *The Motley Fool* and the *Wall Street Journal* and author of *The Psychology of Money*.[1] What Morgan means by this is to save as if you are about to be unemployed, as if the country is about to head into a recession or a bear market. Save like bad things are going to happen. At the same time, invest like an optimist—for the long-term, as if humanity is going to solve problems, companies will become increasingly productive and profitable, and the stock market will do well over time—as if economic prosperity is just around the corner.

Morgan told me that getting rich requires optimism, whether about the stock market, your other investments, or in your own career or business, but that staying rich requires conservative pessimism. It means making sure you leave room for error and enough buffer and low levels of debt so that you can withstand bad times to enjoy the long-term optimism that ultimately will be rewarded.[2]

I want to give you another pro tip. When Kara and I were first married, I handled all things money, including paying the bills and saving for the future, but things began to fall through the cracks. I overcomplicated spending and saving, and what's worse, I didn't enjoy it. (I find that people are good at what they enjoy, and vice versa.) This led to some money disagreements, but we solved the problem with some straight talk. Kara has an uncanny ability to see how pieces fit together, so we agreed that she would take over managing the day-to-day, and I would focus on our long-term investment plan, which was my strength. Getting on the same page financially had a positive impact on our marriage as well as our finances. I'd been driving in two lanes—recklessly in one, it turned out. Once I settled into my own lane and Kara found hers, it became a much smoother, more successful ride for both of us. Find your fast lane—and start winning races.

Working hard for your money isn't enough. Leaving your money to hang out in your checking account won't cut it. Your money deserves better treatment. It's ready and willing to work for you. By investing in the three buckets and the four lanes, you'll teach your money to work hard for you.

Now that you've seen that even investing can be made simple, I want to introduce you to the three levers that will change your relationship with money.

CHAPTER 9

Save More (Lever 1)

A COUPLE OF years ago, I had a startling realization. The last number of my net worth page had jumped dramatically from the year before, so much so that I double- and triple-checked all my account values. But it was correct. Now, what I'm about to tell you may sound very simple. Truly it is, but for me it was also quite profound. Only three levers that I pulled caused a significant increase in my assets.

I call them the Good Money Levers. How and when you pull them will cause your money to work *for* you, not *against* you.

Good Money Levers

- Save more
- Crush your debt
- Earn more

Is it really that easy? Yes. I've shown how the levers work to thousands of clients over the years, explained them, dissected them, tailored them to each individual, and I've seen the levers work wonders. The more I saved, the more debt I paid off, the more my money grew, the more I could give away.

1. The money I saved was invested well and performed well.
2. I aggressively paid down debt (in my case, the mortgage on my house and my business expansion loans).
3. I earned more and saved more.

I love riding the Titan roller coaster at Six Flags Over Texas. Roller coasters are actually simple machines that use levers to help make them run. Each lever plays a crucial job in making the ride work. There's not one more important than the other—all the levers must be operating correctly in order for the roller coaster to perform its intended purpose. Think of my three levers the same way. How you move all of them at the same time determines how hard your money will work for you.

Let's start with Lever 1: Save more.

You work hard for your money, perhaps even at a job that you consider a daily drudge. Even then, your savings gives you a sense of comfort. It's the moat principle. Think of medieval castles. Many of them had a wide band of water around them and, in cartoons at least, crocodiles swimming around. In the event of an enemy attack, marauders would have to trudge through the water, significantly slowing them down and making them more vulnerable. The moat was intended to help insulate the castle's inhabitants from unforeseen attacks.

For most of us, our cash acts as that same kind of buffer. Even if it isn't earning much interest or invested in an aggressive portfolio, it is protecting you and your family from marauders—in this case not human infidels, but unexpected expenses or threats to the health of you or a family member. Stockpiling cash gives us a sense of comfort.

An even better feeling occurs, however, when your money is in motion, particularly that moment when you move from working for your money to your money working for you. If you don't want to think about your money as a moat that surrounds your life, think of it instead as your 100-percent-owned business, and yourself as the CEO of your money.

Bola Sokunbi, founder and CEO of Clever Girl Finance, a personal finance platform that empowers women to achieve real wealth, puts it another way: "It's really building a plan for your money and being the boss, being the CEO, of your dollars and saying, 'Okay, I have this limited amount of money . . . and based on this, based on my expenses, I'm going to be intentional about designating some of this limited amount of money to work for me. . . . That's where the whole idea of paying yourself first comes from. Even if it's a small amount—fifty dollars, twenty dollars, a hundred dollars—it's about being consistent with doing it over time and building the habit of saving so that when you start to earn a ton more money, you're able to save more. . . . It's about building the habit and doing what you can with what you have."[1]

Continuing to speak to this idea of being the boss and the CEO of your dollars, Bola said, "I love for people to think about their finances as their business, their corporation. When you go to work for your employer, you work for a corporation, but in this instance, your dollars are your employees."[2]

Bola offered a good illustration of what she meant that has stuck in my mind. When you go to work at a company, everyone working there has a job. Some people work in marketing, some in sales, some in product creation, but if it's a company that's not doing well, people are likely wasting time. They're in the break room, they're coming to work late, they're slipping in and out of the office without anyone really knowing what they're doing. Bola makes the point that the same applies to your finances. When you're the CEO, you're supposed to be designating specific tasks to your employees and making sure everyone is doing their job well and responsibly. When you are the CEO of your own dollars, you act in precisely the same way. Some of your dollars are focused in the retirement savings department, some for investing, some for paying down debt, some for a cash reserve, and some for having fun and splurging. That's you telling your money what to do.

"When you don't have a plan for your finances, your dollars are hanging out in the break room, having the best time, and not doing anything you need, and they're slipping away, they're leaving work, they're disappearing," Bola told me. "And that's why people look [at their finances] at the end of the month and say, 'Oh my God, I don't know where my money went!'"[3]

Every dollar should have a purpose. You work hard for your money; I want it to work hard for you—beginning today.

Sound impossible? It isn't. Try the following savings strategies:

1. **Cut 20 percent of spending.** Find the waste in your current spending, reduce it, and use it to build assets. (Apply the "back against the wall" approach—if my employer said they had to cut my pay by 20 percent, what would I do?)

2. **Invest with automatic withdrawals.** Increase your retirement contributions to the maximum and get the highest possible company match. Invest your accounts on the basis of your estimated retirement date and what lets you sleep at night.

3. **"Capture and keep" method.** As a kid, I was fascinated with treasure maps. The thought of finding money that once was lost was such a fun idea. Even walking along the sidewalk, if I spotted a penny, I went for it. Finding a quarter was like winning the lottery. As an adult, I have expanded that concept, but it's still a game I enjoy playing,

like calling my service providers each year to find costs I can cut. First, focus on what I call "commoditized cuts." These are services that can be purchased from any number of providers. For example, in Texas, we can choose our electricity provider. Assuming reliability is the same, which it is in Texas, for me that decision is based entirely on cost. I suggest to my clients, "Call your provider and say, 'I'm considering switching service providers to save costs. Do you have a new customer special or any promotional plans I could switch to right now?'" If they say yes, make sure it's the best plan at the best price for you.

Now here's the trick: Take that savings and keep it. Once a savings is found, most people just spend it somewhere else. All they've done is put themselves on a "save and spend program," and they don't move the needle. Instead, capture the money by taking that exact amount you saved and having it automatically deducted from your account and put into savings. Use it to pay off a credit card or a car loan, or to increase your retirement contributions. I used this strategy to pay my house off early.

4. **"Set and Forget."** Set your paycheck so that on the first of the month a certain amount automatically goes into your retirement account, into your savings account, and into your debt-pay-off account. That way you've taken care of your biggest priorities before you spend anything. Whatever money remains can be used for your monthly expenses.

5. **Shift money** saved to pay off high-interest debt and increase retirement savings. (We'll talk more about this in the next chapter.)

6. **Purchase ETFs** (Exchange Traded Funds). They are sound investments set up like miniature index funds, usually less

expensive than mutual funds. (Of course, work with a qualified financial advisor to establish an investment plan based on your specific situation.)

7. **Establish key dates** to mark significant progress. Give yourself incentives and rewards for changing your financial behavior. When you pay off a big debt, celebrate. (But celebrate in cash!)

Bola Sokunbi says two simple words helped her grow her retirement savings by $100,000 in just a few short years. What were those words? "Free money."

"I was the girl who came out of college, just really wanted to focus on saving money and making my parents proud," she explained. "But you know, by 'saving money,' it was really putting money in my bank account, seeing the cash with my eyes whenever I checked. And the whole idea of retirement savings and a 401(k) and all these things I was being told at the first HR meeting was just going over my head. I'm like, 'Who cares about that? I'm not retiring for forty years or something.'"[4]

But then on Bola's next day of orientation, the HR representative described the company's retirement plan and the words that piqued her interest were, "free money." Her employer was offering a 100 percent match of up to 6 percent of Bola's contributions to her retirement plan. "I was like, 'Wait a minute, free money? I'll take that, I'll take whatever it is.' And that was the beginning of me understanding or getting started with investing," she told me. [5] You're putting seeds in the ground with the expectation that they're in good soil and will grow.

Remember, automation is your best friend. When you're making 401(k) contributions, you don't even know it's coming out of your paycheck. You can't even have that mental debate,

"Should I save? Should I not save?" It's happening without your input.

Lara Casey is the founder and CEO of Cultivate What Matters, a company that helps women break down their goals into manageable action steps. She loves to garden with her kids. One of her favorite seeds is shaped like a heart, which is why it's called "Love in a Puff."[6] It grows into a vine and sprouts tiny white flowers and green, papery fruits. I'm not a gardener, but I do know this: seeds kept in their packet will not grow. They need to be planted and watered so they can do their job. Money is the same way. When seeds sprout, when your money is in motion, there's no better feeling. It's the feeling of freedom—that moment where you pivot from you working for your money to your money working for you.

Think of your savings as seeds that can be carefully planted and grow into something beautiful—and you'll see in the next chapter, it all starts with investing.

CHAPTER 10

Crush Your Debt (Lever 2)

I T'S TIME TO pull Lever 2: Crush your debt.

Eliminating debt is ultimately about you taking back control. Do I fault you for getting into debt? No, I'm not here to judge. My goal is to give you the tools to move out and move on. What do I mean by that? Let's say you're just out of college and you have $50,000 of student debt. Or maybe you've had an unexpected medical emergency that has left a $10,000 bill hanging over your head. You have a couple of choices. You can either keep adding to that debt, or say, "No more. I'm going to do whatever it takes to begin chipping away at my debt." Maybe you went through a job layoff or a tough financial patch and racked up credit card debt during the past several years and just can't seem to stop. It's time to look your debt in the face and start taking steps to conquer it. It's held you back for too long—don't let it cost you anymore. Your first step? Be honest with yourself about the amount and origin of the debt. Car? College? Credit card? Write it down along with every interest rate.

It's time to take steps to aggressively eliminate whatever is costing you money and holding you back from lasting wealth.

Here are a few options to consider:

- **List your debts by highest interest rate to lowest.** Then it's attack mode. Don't settle for making the minimum payments. Pile on everything you can. Once the highest interest debt is history, then move to the next one. You'll build momentum and confidence; you'll feel good about taking back more of your hard-earned money.

- **Pay off high-interest credit cards as soon as possible.** Use those savings to build assets. The key is to make a line in the sand and say no more. I had a client one time who went so far as to put his credit cards in a Ziploc bag filled with water and freeze them. Kara and I have been in a similar position when it came to reducing our spending. Every week, we would withdraw cash and place it in labeled envelopes like "groceries" or "gas," and that was all the money we could spend for the week.

- **Make a commitment every quarter to review your progress.** Football has four quarters, God gave us four seasons, companies release quarterly earnings. You're probably seeing a pattern. Four times every year, or every three months, is a good time to press pause—to evaluate your progress. Sports teams and companies adjust along the way and so should you. Measuring leads to momentum.

- **Get an accountability partner.** Whether it's a spouse, significant other, or friend, make a point to regularly check in and talk about any challenges or wins you've experienced. Paying off debt can feel lonely—and this step will help relieve that anxiety and fear.

- **Reward yourself.** Incentives are key here. This kind of strategy harkens back to our nostalgic childhoods when someone said to you, "If you do this, you'll receive this reward." And it worked! You cleaned your room and you got extra screen time. You raked the leaves, and you got $5 to spend as you liked. Now you're all grown up and you can do something similar; only now you're in charge. Say to yourself, "When (not if) I achieve this goal, I'll treat myself." Build it into your budget so you'll have something to motivate you when times are tough and when temptation comes calling.

Kara and I once knew a family who had a different interpretation of being rewarded. Whenever my kids played a game at their house, their dad would always say there was a big prize at the end if you won. Once the game was over, he would say, "Surprise! You get the satisfaction of knowing you won." My kids always thought that was lame—and you might too. If you don't have an incentive you're working toward, it's a lot harder to feel motivated to achieve it. It doesn't have to be big—it can be a clothing item you've been eyeing, going out to eat at a new restaurant, or donating a certain amount to a charity that represents your Generosity Purpose.

I recently played a game with myself. When my podcast launched, I set a goal of a certain number of subscribers. My daughter is a huge baseball fan, and the 2020 World Series was playing near our home in Arlington, Texas. I bought tickets for the family, but then I had an idea. I promised myself that I would not allow myself to go to the game unless I achieved a certain number of subscribers to my podcast. A sense of urgency kicked in. New ideas came to me, and the day before the game, we hit the goal! I had to back myself into a corner to reach it.

Maybe you're in the same boat. It's only when you willingly place yourself in a difficult spot, one in which you do not have a way out except to get out of it yourself, that you will accomplish your goal. And believe me, the day you reach your goal, that is a moment that goes on your personal highlight reel.

The more you sit and think about how the three Good Money Levers of saving more, reducing debt, and earning more can transform your life, the stronger you'll feel a fire start to burn inside you and a new motivation will revolutionize your attitudes toward money and your life.

Here are a few questions to ask yourself:

1. How could I earn more money now?
2. If I had to save 20 percent of my income, could I do it? Or if I had to cut 20 percent of my expenses, could I do it?
3. What are my debts, from the highest interest rate to the lowest?
4. Set a payoff goal now: "I will pay off [insert $ amount and source] by [insert date]."

And now (drum roll), for everyone's favorite lever, number three: Earn more now!

CHAPTER 11

Earn More Now (Lever 3)

THERE IS ONE distinct belief that separates people who build real, lasting wealth and people who spend, spend, spend. It's that they treat money as a river, not a pond. Don't get me wrong; I love the water and taking a swim on a hot Texas day. But at the pond near my house, water that is stagnant and not cared for attracts mosquitoes. It forms an unattractive film on top and begins to develop a stench. Many people think of money the same way. It's in a contained source, only to be found by the rich people who own big companies. It's dirty and smelly.

Real wealth builders imagine money as a continuously flowing river, rather than a standing pond of water. There's not a limited supply. Money flows where value goes. It is meant to be in motion, so in my world, money is pure, clean, and refreshing. Instead of imagining it sitting in a pond, waiting to be used as crud forms on top, think of it, used wisely, as a continuously flowing river that can be diverted to feed multiple crops—yourself, your family, others you love, and those you want to help.

I often hear from people who feel like they're off track and they'll never catch up. No. If you take away one message from this chapter, from this book, it's that you have *choices*. It's in your power to change your financial reality, to earn more, save more, and give more. When you start believing that money is a river that flows where value is, the ways you can earn more are endless, which brings us to this third lever.

Remember the number you wrote down when we walked through the Good Money Framework? It might be 25 percent or 50 percent higher than your current income. Earning more looks different for everyone, but I want to share some Good Money Moves you can start implementing today:

Option 1: Treat your job as if you were an entrepreneur.

Remember that feeling you get on Sunday about 4:00 p.m.? You're having a great day, but suddenly, "Oh, tomorrow's Monday and I've got to start this treadmill all over again." Instead, start thinking of your job like you're a business owner. When you do, you'll learn skills that will prepare you to create your own venture or side hustle, or even propel you higher at the company you work for right now. As an employee, you should always be asking yourself, "How can I increase sales, boost productivity, or innovate to make a product or service better?"

I think of Kelsey, who, after six years working for a local insurance company, felt the door closing on any advancement opportunities. While the lead sales representative worked with clients face-to-face, Kelsey was known for how well she supported customers. In a performance evaluation, her boss shared some aggressive growth goals and asked for her feedback on ways they could serve more clients. Kelsey quickly recognized an opportunity to both help the business flourish and grow her paycheck. She understood these clients, and who better to work with them than her? A few days later, she presented a thoughtful proposal to her boss. She asked him to pay her to get licensed, then transition 25 percent of his clients to her as their sales rep, which would free up her boss to bring in more business. She asked for an incentive based on new business opportunities that she identified. Her boss loved the idea! She was thinking like a business owner while working inside someone else's company. No matter your job, there are always ways to make your products, services, processes, and customer experience better. Empower yourself in the job you're in right now and think about new ways to make your current job better.

Option 2: Add value
to grow your company's revenue.

The way to make more money is to add more value. I need you to understand one key component: whatever you're paid right now is what the economy is saying you're worth right now. If you think about pro athletes who get huge contracts, you may think, "How can they be paid that much?" It's simply because the economy says, "That's what they're worth." When you add value to the company, your value goes up. Do this by asking your boss for more responsibility (and nailing it!), increasing sales, reducing expenses, or getting a new certification or degree.

Debbie's decision to join the startup engineering firm was both exciting and exhilarating, but two years into it, while most other people had been promoted, she was feeling stuck. She was growing disillusioned with her future. "Derrick," she told me, "I want to make more money, but I'm not sure how."

Together, Debbie and I created a two-pronged plan with which she would approach her boss. Bur first, she did some due diligence. In her current position, she didn't have any bonus or commission potential, but as she talked to a few salespeople, she gained a much better understanding of the company's sales goals and compensation structure. She then set up an appointment with the CEO. First, she asked him, "If I get an advanced certification and I can demonstrate how that would help make the company more money, could I earn a salary increase?" The CEO was impressed with the way she positioned herself. It wasn't just, "I want more money," but, "If I do this and help the company make more money, could I then get a part of that?" Then the second part blew the CEO away. "As I talked to our salespeople," she told him, "I realized we must know other business owners who could use what our company produces. What if you gave a finder's fee to me and other employees who refer business to the sales department?" Well, this was eye-opening for the CEO, and on the spot he agreed to give her a $5,000 salary increase upon completion of the advanced certification (which would reimburse the cost of the certification). Plus, he agreed to give her and the rest of the team a referral fee if they produced a lead who became a customer.

Debbie continued to explain how she would stay motivated to get this certificate and connect the company with other business owners. She told the CEO that there was a week-long summer camp at the local university for junior high students interested in STEM (Science, Technology, Engineering, and Math). It was something Debbie wished was available when she was younger and she wanted to provide scholarships for ten students to go. The CEO was so impressed when Debbie presented her Generosity Purpose that he offered to support the cause as well. It was a win-win all the way around.

Michael Hyatt, CEO and author of *Win at Work and Succeed at Life*, once told me, "The most popular 'radio station' in the world is WIIFM—'What's In It For Me?' People don't act for your best interests; they act for their own best interests. So I don't care whether you're trying to sell a board member or you're trying to sell the banker or you're trying to sell a customer or you're trying to sell an employee—you've got to enter into their world. You've got to see it from their perspective and sell it from the perspective of how it's gonna benefit them. If you can do that, you can sell anything—I don't care if it's an idea or if it's a product or if it's a service."[1]

Debbie knew this well. She was able to clearly communicate to the CEO the value she could bring to the company, herself, and the causes she believed in—and her salary increase reflected her persuasive conviction.

Option 3: Start a side hustle.

If you're not satisfied with your salary and your promotion possibilities are limited, a side venture could be developed into a business of your own. We've learned during COVID-19 that most people are simply one global event away from losing their job or taking a pay cut. Let me be candid with you: if you're working for someone else, this can be a dangerous situation because you are reliant on them and only them for your income. You want to be a creator of money, not only the receiver of it—and starting a side hustle is a great way to get started.

Entrepreneur and real estate coach Ryan Pineda told me his first side hustle was being a realtor, then he became a substitute teacher, then he got into couch flipping, and finally he started flipping houses. He says, "There are a lot of side hustles, like my own, that will pay more than your job. If you just take the risk and go all in at the side hustle, you can have a business."[2] Often some of the best side hustles emerge either from what you're already doing in your full-time job or from something you're really good at and enjoy.

Sheila and Dan loved to travel, especially when their trips involved something adventuresome, like deep-sea diving. Their holidays and vacations were planned months in advance, and the planning brought them nearly as much joy as the trips themselves. As more friends and colleagues asked them for trip planning tips, a part-time travel business was born. Sheila's virtual job as a marketing consultant and Dan's at-home job in software sales afforded them some flexibility. Working during lunch breaks, evenings, and weekends let Sheila and Dan help others see the world—and pack their own retirement fund with the fees they charged.

Craig was an engineer by day and a poet by night. His full-time job paid the bills, but writing filled his soul. He ended up with a book deal. Reducing his lifestyle, he took early retirement and turned his side hustle into a rewarding part-time job.

There are limitless side hustles out there—brainstorm, get creative, and pursue something you're good at. Perceive a need and fulfill it. Your goal? Let your side hustle become your main income—and have fun doing it.

CHAPTER 12

How to Ask for a Raise

THIS SIMPLEST OPTION, asking for a raise, might feel the scariest of all, but have no fear—I'm about to reveal the best strategies you need to get the raise, promotion, or bonus you deserve.

We've discussed how your job is not all about the money, that it's important to feel good about what you're doing. But sometimes it *is* about the money. After all, you have to *make* money to *give* money away—to fulfill your Generosity Purpose.

In order to start earning more, saving more, and giving more, you may have to make some changes in your job situation. But before you do, ask yourself:

- In your job, are you communicating your value?
- How confident do you feel asking for a raise?
- What about a promotion?
- Have you considered additional training to better position yourself for success?
- Are you worthy of making more money? (Yes!)

Many people are hurting right now. I know that for many Americans, it's hard to put food on the table, and I understand where they're coming from. But I believe people should not be handed the crumbs off the table by the government; I want them to have a seat at the table. It's your job to add so much value to people that you're worth more than the minimum wage—far more. If you live a minimum wage life, you're going to have minimum opportunities. You're going to make minimum money and have minimum relationships. It doesn't have to be that way.

There's a gap between you wanting to earn more money and the person in charge of the decision to pay you more. I'm going to help you close that gap. While it's been made to be a deeply complex issue, it's actually quite simple. Two words are battling each other: *value* and *fairness*. Take the example of high-producing athletes who are paid a boatload of cash because of the value society places on what they do. They put fans in seats, sell concessions and sports memorabilia, and help the team win the coveted championship. Let's say they get paid $4 million per year.[1] Now let's take you. You work hard at your job, but you don't feel like you're paid what you're worth.

At the risk of you slamming this book closed in disgust, I know you don't want me to sugarcoat this. Based on what you're currently getting paid, you're not adding as much value to your company as the athlete is to their team. That's not fair, is it? You and the athlete both work hard, but they're earning fifty or one hundred times what you're receiving. Now the point I'm making is not for you to suit up and pursue an athletic career. You won't hear me holding you back, but I hope I'm not the first to tell you, that ship has likely already sailed. What I am telling you is this: you must add more value to your company and your company's clients or customers. Otherwise, the salary you earn now will likely not change unless you decide to change jobs. Money chases value. Add value to an enterprise, and its money will chase you.

Your first option may well be to consider negotiating for a higher salary, but there's a right way to do that. Ramit Sethi, author of *I Will Teach You to Be Rich*, told me that he learned about negotiating on his visits to the markets in India, where both his parents were born. "We learned that you can ask for something, when appropriate, and the other person is under no obligation to give it to you," he explains. "But sometimes just asking, and doing it correctly, can give you major advantages."[2]

Ramit believes this applies to almost every area of life, including salary negotiations. When looking for additional compensation, he says that the first key is to understand whether you are underpaid; a lot of people in his I Will Teach You to Be Rich community are underpaid by $5,000, $10,000, even $20,000 per year. "You can go to sites like Payscale.com or Salary.com, and you can plug in your information and see how you are paid [compared to similar jobs in your field]," he suggests. "That's a big revelation to people when they realize, 'Oh, my God, I've been *dramatically* underpaid.'"[3]

Ramit's second piece of advice is to think strategy. "So the typical approach for salary negotiation is, people think they're gonna kick down their boss's door and just put their hand out and say, 'Give me some money.' And then they go, 'My boss will never go for it!' Yeah, of course not. Who would go for someone going, 'Give me money'? That's not how it works."[4]

If you feel like you are underpaid, the first thing to do is to look inward, rather than outward. Inquire how to help your boss achieve his or her goals and show your willingness to be a valuable and profitable team member. Few people ask their superiors how they can help, and those who do automatically stand out. Become indispensable. Develop the ability to handle multiple tasks. Volunteer for projects, especially those that are stimulating and in your areas of strength. Talk to your boss; make sure your boss appreciates you and feels like you're doing a good job. Create income opportunities for your company. Identify what you're good at and look for opportunities to take advantage of those strengths. Add value to your work. When you add value, you make yourself worth more to your employer. And finally, ask to be paid what you believe you are worth. When you add value or create revenue for your employer, you deserve to be compensated accordingly.

Ramit suggests setting up a meeting with your boss to ask what it would take to become a top performer. Then once you're crystal clear on the answer, have it in your mind to exceed those goals in the coming months. Say to your boss, "Assuming I hit all these [objectives], I'd like to discuss a compensation adjustment, but first let me work on these things."[5] Then you spend the next four to six months working on these objectives, so when you walk in for your review, you've already nailed it.

"You've already been communicating [with your boss] for the last six months," Ramit explains. "You have your data from the websites, and you can have an informed discussion about your salary. This is how many, many, many of my readers negotiate ten- or fifteen-thousand-dollar raises. And so, you can do it, but you need to approach it in the right way."[6]

In other words, first add value, then ask for the raise you obviously deserve. "When it comes to negotiating, it's a dance," Ramit explained. He added, "Your boss is under no obligation to pay you more [just because you ask]; similarly, you are under no obligation to stay. If you find that the market tells you you are worth more, you could leave."[7]

But be careful about treating this as a short-term strategy. Ramit reminds us that compensation can be about other factors in addition to money. "You might be getting compensated with other things, like you love your coworkers or you're learning a lot of skills. There are lots of reasons to stay or to leave, but simply saying, 'I'm underpaid, please pay me more'—that's not persuasive."[8] Yes, you could threaten your boss with leaving unless you get a raise, and if your leaving puts your boss in a bind, she may agree to your demands. But that's like putting a Band-Aid on a compound fracture. It doesn't solve your long-term problem.

Dan Miller, author of *48 Days to the Work You Love*, among other bestsellers, agrees. "I don't encourage anybody, 'Hey, just quit your job,'" he told me. "But capture those ideas that you've had that have been recurring. A lot of what's happened right now, where people are in this state of insecurity and uncertainty, it's brought back to the surface ideas that have been dormant for twenty years. *Man, when I was eighteen years old I had this idea—I never did anything with it. I just got caught up in the expected, and here I am twenty years later.* This is a time to go back and revisit those ideas. I'm not talking about being some radical inventor who, you're gonna come up with the next Hula-Hoop or Frisbee. That may be the case, but it may be something more ordinary than that, that you just do in a really, really excellent way."[9]

Dan breaks our working life into decades. "There are predictable kinds of patterns that we go through," he explains. "In our twenties, essentially, we're *learning*—that's a learning decade. Thirties is usually *experimenting*—you're kind of sorting things out, what fits you. Forties we call *mastering*. This is the decade when you focus on those things that you hung on to, where you're really developing your skills, becoming an expert. Fifties are *reaping*. You're really maximizing the benefits of where you are at that point. Sixties are usually *guiding*, seventies, you're leaving a *legacy*. And we can go on from there. I like to go all the way up to like, where somebody's a sage, where you're respected just for the wisdom, reflection on life that you offer."[10]

Dan's point is if someone is in their forties and realizes they may have made a mistake and may want to choose something different, they don't need to go back to when they were a teenager and start thinking about all those same possibilities. Now they have the wisdom of experience to guide them toward making a good decision for moving forward much more quickly. At the same time, someone in their sixties may decide they want to learn a musical instrument, or a new way of investing. No matter your age, the possibilities are endless—but it's time to make some changes now.

Tell yourself that in the next thirty days, you're going to make three courageous money moves:

1. I'm going to talk to my boss and ask him point blank, "What would it take to have my salary increased?"
2. I'm going to take on more responsibility.
3. I'm going to sign up for additional training that will help me advance in my career.

You'll see that just writing all this down or saying it aloud will begin to stem the tide of money negativity and unleash the ability to earn more, save more, and ultimately give more. Gradually, you'll begin to take small risks and build true money momentum. Give yourself a deadline of thirty days. A self-imposed sense of urgency will lead to quicker results. Then delve a little further with a few other questions. Can you move out of your current role but remain in your place of employment? Are you able to take on more responsibility to boost your pay? Or maybe it's time to start a side gig to determine whether you have a viable alternative.

If the answer is no, then ask yourself if it's time to jump ship. You make more money based on the value you create—and it might be time to look for other opportunities.

But wait just a minute. What about those who feel stuck in a fixed-salary job, or find themselves squarely in the middle of an increasingly "nontraditional" economy? If you're not employed in a conventional professional environment, you may feel you're not in a position to ask for more money. That's understandable. If you're working in a field solely based on seniority or a set pay-range, or you're working part-time, developing a side gig in a field in which you have an expertise, or changing jobs or even professions, asking for a raise might not seem particularly relevant.

Think again. As I write these words, we're witnessing one of the greatest employment power shifts in history. Some call it the Great Resignation; others, a nationwide labor shortage. By whatever name, it's a moment in time when, in many fields, employees have more cards to play than ever before. Quality people are at a premium, and employers are recognizing their need to provide new kinds of incentives to retain and attract the best workers.

This is at least partly true in every field. Not only are hourly wages being increased, but employers are offering low-risk yet valuable benefits, like work-from-home options, childcare flexibility, and enhanced vacation and maternity/paternity policies. For these same reasons, middle managers, too, have more options than ever before in deciding whether to jump to a competitor for a larger salary or better benefits.

You may think you're working in a field that doesn't lend itself to an immediate bump in salary, but that might not necessarily be true. Let's say you're a teacher, for example. You walk into your boss's office, in this case the principal's office, and you tell her you'd like to be paid more. But she tells you her hands are tied, that either because of union contracts or budget restrictions, she has no leeway to give a single teacher a raise, regardless of merit.

So what do you do? I'll tell you. You think outside the box and take your expertise and marketing to people in your field who will find it valuable.

Start by taking a sheet of paper and writing out the best ways you, as a teacher, encourage your students to their highest level of success. What are the most effective strategies your experience has told you are most effective? You may even want to ask colleagues or friends to identify the skills you have that make you unique.

This becomes the first ingredient in a recipe you can share with others. Think about how valuable the lessons you've learned over the years would be to a new teacher. You're the experienced person who has gone through the potholes and joys of teaching and can share that knowledge so others can achieve their own success more quickly.

Next, brainstorm and write down the different ways you might be able to monetize your expertise. Maybe a way to get started is to speak at teacher conferences or use teacher organizations and social media to advertise your services as a coach. Newbie teachers might be interested, but you can also take advantage of the definite trend of more and more parents who are interested in paying qualified people with a track record to help their children academically and to prepare for college. You may end up creating a separate revenue stream for yourself, while at the same time benefiting a cause you believe in, namely helping to train the next generation of teachers to be the best they can be.

The bottom line? No matter who you are or what kind of job you currently hold, this may be the ideal time to investigate alternatives.

CHAPTER 13

Burn the Ships

DOING A GOOD job at your place of employment, while at the same time developing skills and increasing your value, can definitely be an effective Good Money strategy. But it's not always enough. Sometimes if you're miserable in your job, you just have to "pull a Cortés" and burn the ships behind you.

Pull a Cortés? Burn your ships? Well, not literally, of course, but you can take your cue from the Spanish conquistador Hernán Cortés, who in 1519 arrived in the New World with six hundred soldiers. On the first day, he sent a clear message to his men by destroying his ships.[1] What was the message? There was no turning back; the only way was forward.

Trapped in a job you abhor, sometimes you just have to take the plunge and go out on your own. Sure, you can find another job, but more often than not, that's not going to solve your problem. Besides, salaried employment isn't typically the most direct way to wealth, and remember, the focus of this book is for you to make more money so you can do more good in the world. The more money you make, the more good you can do, and being miserable in a job is not going to help anyone.

Here's the reality: If you're not getting what you want right now, like the amount of money you feel you deserve or the job you believe you should have, and you just feel stuck doing the same thing, it's time to make a change.

Is it risky? Yes. Is it bold? Yes. Can it make all the difference? Yes.

I believe the timing of *Good Money Revolution* couldn't be better. Sure, it's great to make money. You go to your job, get a paycheck, and pay the mortgage. But isn't there more to life than that? Is there a way for you to feel like you are actually making a difference in the world while you work hard to earn that paycheck?" Yes. That's what I'm digging into.

You'll know when the time is right. It might not be easy to admit it to yourself, and it might mean taking a big risk, but trust your instincts. Build on your talents. After identifying your strengths, position yourself to do more of *that* type of work. Or start it as a side business. Don't wait until you retire to begin something new. That way, you'll be retiring *to* something, not just *from* something.

Where you are is where you are. Your next move is your money move. Until your life is over, there is opportunity. (Don't die before you're dead.) It's not easy, but you can do it. I like Michael Hyatt's definition of an entrepreneur as "someone who solves problems at a profit."[2] He should know; he's written five bestsellers and built a successful company. And remember the famous note of caution (or is it encouragement?) from the screenwriter, William Goldman: "Nobody knows anything," which means your dream can come true as easily as anyone else's.[3]

Marc Randolph, a serial entrepreneur and the cofounder and first CEO of Netflix, clearly agrees with this notion, as do all the entrepreneurs I've encountered. "If someone has an idea, I'll be the first to tell you, 'That'll never work,'" he told me. "But the trick is that should not stop you from starting. . . . Anyone who tells you, 'Oh, that's not gonna work,' they have no idea what they're talking about. They are no more informed or less informed than you are. They're guessing. And the only way to find out whether your idea is a good one or a bad one is to try."[4]

Even the large companies you know and love didn't get big without struggle or even serious missteps. Marc reminded me that it took a decade before Netflix expanded its business of mailing out other studio's films to streaming its own original programming. "Your job is not to come up with the perfect idea," he told me. "[It's] to take a flawed idea, to figure out a quick and easy and cheap way to start, and begin the process of iteration. You take your idea, you collide it with reality, you learn how your initial assumptions were wrong, but you're gathering insights now about, 'Wait a minute, maybe *that* might work.'"[5]

Lara Casey is an avid gardener and often uses her hobby as a metaphor for her business philosophy. "All I can do is to do my part," she told me, "and that is to literally plant the seed in the ground and trust that it's gonna do what it was created to do. But can I control that? No, but that's where I think we get stuck . . . holding on to these proverbial seeds in our lives and feeling like, 'Well, if I open my hand here, and if I release this into the ground, what if it doesn't grow?' And my challenge to everyone is, 'What if it *does* grow?' You have to take a risk for the things that really matter or else you're gonna feel stuck."[6]

Dan Miller says it's important to look more inward and less outward when it comes to finding your dream job. "People are too quick to look for external solutions," he told me. "'What's the best major in college? Who's hiring? What about Uncle Bob who worked at General Motors for thirty years and ended up pretty comfortable?' So they look for external solutions. Whereas 85 percent of the process of having the confidence about proper direction in your career comes from looking inward. *Look inward.* Figure out what's unique about yourself in terms of skills and abilities, personality traits, values, dreams, passions. Then you have a clear focus and an authentic focus—15 percent is the application, that's actually the easy part, but people too quickly go to that. So they try to superimpose something on them that's not really an authentic fit. And then they just try to tough it out and make it work."[7]

Dan is saying that too many people are putting Band-Aids on wounds that never heal. "If it's not a fit, you don't naturally work harder, faster, or more efficiently," he explains. "It's like driving from Nashville to San Francisco and you make a wrong turn. Now you're headed toward New Orleans. You don't just speed up and go faster or drive more efficiently. You're on the wrong road. The same is true with planning your life."

Whether it's burning the ships and stepping away from a job you've held for years or scheduling a meeting with your boss to review what it will take to achieve a raise or promotion, take one step of action today toward your ideal life. Nothing big—just one step. It can be the difference between renting your life and owning it. It's time to take the plunge.

CHAPTER 14

Taking the Plunge

I DON'T HAVE a lot of regrets in my life, but there are two that I think about often. They both taught me the same lesson—to act on what I know is the right thing for me to do for myself, my family, and the world on which I'm trying to have an impact. They're both dreamlike in my consciousness because while they were both seemingly inconsequential incidents, they taught me a valuable lesson.

The first incident occurred at the age of 13 while attending a concert at our local church with my dad. We arrived late and it looked like every seat was taken. As we surveyed the room, a door opened to our left and in walked a group of people who confidently began walking to the front of the large room.

I felt a tug, not on my sleeve, but in my gut. You know the feeling—the one you get inside when you know you should do something but you hold back. I had an immediate sense of urgency to follow that confident group to the front of the stage. I didn't know where we would end up sitting, or if we'd get busted for following them, but in that moment I was thirsty for adventure. Heck, we might have walked down to the front and discovered there wasn't room for us. That would have been embarrassing, but we also might have enjoyed the concert from the very front. All I knew was that in the moment, I froze and didn't bet on myself. My dad and I ended up sitting in seats that needed binoculars. To this day, I know we would have been no worse off if I had followed my instincts, and that I'd definitely have a better story to tell.

My other regret happened more recently, and it showed me that I hadn't really learned the lesson from that time at church with my dad many years earlier. This time, it was at a baseball game with my son Conner. I had promised each of my children that for their fourteenth birthday, I'd take them on a trip to any-where they wanted to go, within reason of course, just the two of us. Conner chose a trip to Miami to do some deep-sea fishing and see a Marlins game. Conner loves baseball, and his favorite player at the time was the Marlins' right fielder, Giancarlo Stanton. In art class Conner had drawn a picture of Stanton, which he hoped to get autographed.

As a splurge, I bought us seats right behind the dugout. We got to the game early, picture in hand, and as the players filed into the dugout, there he was, Giancarlo Stanton. All it would have taken was calling out his name and we would have had a lifetime memory. Instead, just like in the church, I held back. I was guilty of being concerned about what other people might think of me. I've always regretted not taking that risk. The only upside is how much enjoyment my kids get hearing how their dad goofed up. They'll always listen to those kinds of stories.

Part of my reluctance at the church and at the ball game was fear of what others would think, and the other part was fear of being embarrassed. The fear of the unknown, of what might happen, most of which is only imagined and, in most cases, never comes true. It's that fear inside your own head that is trapping you—that fear of your past, of what you think might occur or of what the voice in your head is telling you *will* occur. Instead,

turn those thoughts around. Send yourself a continuously loop-
ing message that you should reject your well-worn path of dashed
money dreams so you can have a positive impact on the world.

As for me, never again. I vowed in the future never to ignore
that "tug," and a few years later I took the plunge to burn my own
ships.

Each July for the past several years, I've taken a sabbatical.
It's a week-long period alone for me to think, pray, and journal.
I ask myself how I can be a better father, leader, husband, and
business owner. It's a time to tamp down the noise, turn up the
dreams, and resurface ideas in my head that need to break free. If
I'm going to run fast for fifty-one weeks a year, I need to take at
least one week to plan the race.

Leading up to the sabbatical a few years ago, my plan was to
strategize on how to significantly grow my financial planning and
investment business. I thrive on growth and had identified Nashville as my next target. I'd been introduced to a man who knew
all the advisors in town and was willing to make introductions for
me. One day I'll never forget, he suddenly challenged me with a
question: "Derrick, why do you want to keep growing your business?" The question stung and stopped me cold. I responded that
I wanted to keep growing because I enjoyed the challenge.

But back in the hotel room, I knew the question deserved a
deeper answer, one that I promised myself to think about further
during my sabbatical. On the first morning, I typed out a list of
all the things I enjoyed doing, and how I could do more of them,
more frequently. To be honest, financial planning wasn't on the
list.

One thing I enjoyed the most was appearing on television as
a voice of reason making complex financial topics easy to understand. I loved my interviews on FOX News, CNN, CNBC, PBS,
and all the broadcast networks. It is such an adrenaline rush when

I help people make sense of their problems and when I'm able to add real value to their lives.

I had a problem, however. Due to the approval requirements at my national investment firm, it was very difficult to accept network television opportunities. Often, by the time I got the go-ahead from my firm, the news outlets had moved on. At one point, a national television outlet offered me a regular segment, but my firm said no.

I had a choice to pursue my passions, not only to appear on television more regularly, but to pursue other dreams as well, like hosting a financial podcast or authoring a common-sense personal finance book. When I studied the list of things I enjoyed, I got excited, because right in front of me were the things I desired to do the most. The idea of helping people earn more, save more, and give more, and bringing that vision to a national stage excited me to no end. It took my breath away. I loved my business and serving my clients, some for as long as twenty-five years. But I knew that to expand my circle of influence would demand that I make the hard decision to sell my business so I could take my message to a broader audience.

I called my wife, Kara, and asked if she was sitting down. I told her what I had discovered about myself, that I had decided to sell the firm but to give myself two years to build up the value and help transition my clients. What she said shocked me. "I think you should sell it now," Kara said. "You've talked about wanting to pursue something else for quite some time. We're in this together, so let's do it."

Then *I* was the one who needed to sit down. I was reminded of one of my favorite scenes in the movie *The Shawshank Redemption*, when Ellis Boyd "Red" Redding is finally released from jail. "I find I'm so excited I can barely sit still or hold a thought in my head," he says. "I think it's the excitement only a free man can feel, a free man at the start of a long journey whose conclusion is uncertain."[1]

I didn't jump because I disliked my job. On the contrary, I loved it, but I was ready for something new. In fact, one of the most difficult, gut-wrenching decisions I've ever made was to sell my practice in order to pursue a new passion. I built a financial planning practice over twenty-five years and loved it. I loved helping people make money and achieve their goals. It was such a meaningful profession for me, but something happened. In my case, my inspiration came from an emerging voice in culture today that says, *If you have money, you're bad, and if you have a lot of money, you're really bad.* I know many people feel money is not good for them or for anyone else. They may have grown up in an environment where it was the haves against the have-nots. I launched a podcast and wrote this book to push hard against that argument that says, *If you have money, you're bad.* Instead, I believe money is good, and good people should have more of it.

You may be wrestling with change right now. It can be scary. I understand. Choosing to step away from great clients who loved what I did for them to pursue something new without a job description was scary. Because of the long-term nature of so many trusting relationships, I decided to call each client individually. Every conversation was painful, like ripping off a Band-Aid. During each phone call, a videotape played in my mind of all the experiences we had shared. Understand that not everyone will applaud your dream or your decision to "burn the ships." I was questioned deeply by friends and colleagues. You may expect those who know you the best will be the most supportive, but that wasn't always the case. Some asked if I had been sober when I had made the decision, or if I was having a mid-life crisis. One woman suggested I not sell the business, but buy a Corvette instead.

You reach a point, a fork in the road, where you have to choose. Deep down you realize that the path you're on is a well-worn, familiar one. To be true to yourself, to give yourself the opportunity to live the life you've always wanted and to make the money you feel you deserve, you may need to begin a new adventure.

I'm reminded of the snow globes I had as a kid at Christmas. I loved to turn a globe over and watch the snow settle at the bottom, then flip it to see the snow gently float down and resettle. It occurred to me, even at a young age, that the people portrayed in the globe are stuck in their bubble. The snow globe was a metaphor for something bigger: only after stepping out of our comfortable places can we see things in a different light.

Even celebrities you know and love sometimes step back, reassess, and make major changes in their lives, and even for them, that decision can impact their personal finances. When I spoke with the actor Matthew McConaughey, I was impressed by his determination to reboot his career. By 2009, he had a string of hits behind him where he had played the romantic lead in films like *The Wedding Planner*, *How to Lose a Guy in 10 Days*, *Failure to Launch*, and *Ghosts of Girlfriends Past*. "I was the go-to rom-com guy," he told me. "They were doing well at the box office, I was enjoying doing them, and it got to be a time where I would pick up the next rom-com script and look at it, read it, and go, 'Oh, that's a good one . . . but I feel like I can do that tomorrow morning.'" McConaughey continued, "But then I was like, 'Well, wait a minute. I want to do some work that I look at and I read the script and I go, *Whoa, I don't know what the heck I'm gonna do with this, but I can't wait to find out.*'"[2]

Matthew stuck to his guns. "While the rom-coms were, yes, filling my bank account, and my bank account was full enough for me to say, 'I'm going to stop work,' my soul's account was in the debit section," he told me.[3] "We look at ourself, and we do our inventory, and we say, 'Wait a minute, I'm just dominating my career, but, ah my home life is not healthy, or my spiritual life is not healthy, or I'm not taking care of myself. It's all about relationships. We have relationships with our career, we have relationships with our loved ones, we have relationships with our past, our future. So, sometimes we have a relationship that's going really well in our life when another one's in the debit section.... If we can keep our soul's account full while having our bank account full, that's the honey hole. That's when we're like, 'Okay, I'm in the sweet spot.'"[4]

Matthew says once he was "unbranded" by Hollywood he was able to start fresh. After not working for twenty months, he suddenly starred in another string of hits, this time dramas like *The Lincoln Lawyer*, *Killer Joe*, *Mud*, and *Magic Mike*. He won an Academy Award for his role in *Dallas Buyers Club*. His patience paid off. Do you think he would have won an Oscar for his role in *Surfer, Dude*?

Okay, that's Matthew McConaughey. You're not a movie star. Neither am I. But I think we all face a similar challenge: feeling pigeonholed in one area of our lives. All big ideas start with small steps. Small steps can lead to big rewards.

In my experience with thousands of clients over the years, for those who arrived every morning at a job that made them miserable, their job was often making them sick. As an investment advisor, sometimes I felt my job traveled into life coach territory. More than once I nudged clients away from an employment situation that was increasingly, over a period of years, having a negative impact on their health.

It's like the frog in the kettle, an image I've never really liked to think about. You know the story. If you put a frog in a pot of water on the stove and suddenly turn the heat to high, it will jump out of the pot. But if you only gradually increase the heat, the frog will just sit there. Eventually it will boil to death, not sensing the gradual changes.

Like the frog, too many people stay in jobs because of the paycheck they come to count on. They don't see how it's impacting their health and, often, their relationships. I've counseled clients who gradually became distant from their family and friends, not so much because of the hours they worked, but because they started to dread having to go into the office each day, resenting every minute. Eventually their resentment spilled over into their personal relationships, whether it was intended or not.

"If you don't truly love [your work] . . . try to find the love in it," says Jon Gordon. "If that doesn't work, well then you've got to find something that really does bring you love and joy, that will bring you alive, make you sing, and make you want to show up every day to be great at it."[5]

My fear today is that you will continue on this path of a job you dislike, leading into a career you despise that drains your joy, and then into a retirement that feels meaningless. You have one life to live. It's time to live it well.

CHAPTER 15

Failure as Fertilizer

I WANT TO warn you of an enemy that you are sure to meet: failure. Dealing with failure is just as important as dealing with money. We often see entrepreneurs on television or social media and think, *They have it all figured out, I wish I could be like that.* But that line of thinking holds more people back from achieving their goals and dreams than almost anything else. The reality is, your favorite entrepreneurs have all battled tremendous failure or embarrassment—and they know it's a part of the process. After all, it's called research and development.

Here's what researchers have discovered: successful people fail *more* and fail *faster* than other people.[1] When someone begins to create a new product or take action on an exciting idea, they test it and it fails. Then they test it again and it fails. And again and again.

But here's the key difference: They quickly assess what went wrong and ask themselves what they would do differently. Then they try it again and repeat that process until they reach their goal. You see, between the words *start* and *finish* is the word *fail*. The quicker you embrace failure as part of the journey, the sooner you will find yourself among the ranks of the successful.

Billionaire and founder of Paychex, Tom Golisano, told me of the time he took his office staff to a restaurant. When the waiter came back with his American Express card, it was cut in two. "Fortunately, that steakhouse was a client," he explained, "and I asked the owner if he would just take credit for his payroll processing . . . against my bill, and he said yes. But it's one of life's embarrassing moments."[2]

Surprises will always occur, and plans don't always go according to plan. Problems will arise—job loss, medical issues, natural disasters, family changes—all of which can destroy your financial landscape. Anticipate these possibilities and plan for those you can't anticipate. The important thing is not to lose everything when a crisis occurs. Instead, understand that problems will occur, anticipate them, and find ways to control them. Then make whatever changes are necessary. Going into the process, successful people know failure is inevitable.

Jesse Cole wrote a book called *Find Your Yellow Tux*, which is his way of saying find the best version of yourself—the one thing that makes you stand out—then amplify it. Jesse did just that when he transformed the Savannah Bananas into the most successful minor league baseball team in America, but he didn't do it by spending endless hours on strategy. He did it by trying various ideas to see which ones worked best. Many failed. He told me, "Some promotions on the field, like 'Living Piñata,' where we put an intern in a turtle costume and had kids hit him with plastic bats while throwing candy—that didn't work that well."[3]

We all make mistakes. I've made plenty of them, and I am sure I'll have a ton more to make in the future. But what allows me to continue to be successful is learning from those mistakes. Lara Casey says she treats failure as fertilizer. I love that phrase. "I don't know about you," she told me, "but sometimes when something doesn't go my way, it really fires me up. I'm like, 'Ah, okay, well that was a major flop; I totally could have done that better. I'm going to use that frustration as fuel to move forward on something better in the future.'"[4]

Michael Hyatt guides hundreds of entrepreneurs in his BusinessAccelerator coaching program. After COVID-19 hit, he asked them, "Do we have more problems today than we had a month ago?" And, of course, they all said, "Absolutely." "Isn't that awesome?" Michael told them. "Because there's more opportunity for us. If we'll embrace it, if we'll be innovative, if we'll lean into this, there's more opportunity for us now than there was a month ago."[5]

It feels like an oxymoron: failure fuels progress.

When it comes to our own money, it's easy to hold ourselves to a higher standard, so when we make a mistake, we think to ourselves, *Well, I guess I'm just not that good with money.* Let's say you finally took the plunge after hearing about a hot stock that your friend made a killing on, only to get in too late and lose money. Maybe you felt embarrassed and decided the stock market just wasn't for you. Or after doing your due diligence, you bought a used car and just a few months later, major engine repairs were needed that weren't covered under warranty. The thought that you're not good at buying cars hung heavy on your psyche.

Here's a dose of reality for you: things happen. One mistake, two mistakes, three mistakes, more. Heck, none of these mistakes define you or your ability to make good decisions in the future. The secret is to learn from each mistake. In fact, while you're in the midst of the disaster, jot down a few notes to yourself about what you'll do differently next time. If you're going to be successful, it simply means that you're going to make more mistakes than the average person. Fortunately, you expected them, learned from them, and kept moving forward. Remember, we all come with a reset button. Successful people press it often.

One of my favorite stories comes from Marshall Goldsmith's book *Mojo: How to Get It, How to Keep It, How to Get It Back If You Lose It*. The story tells about legendary musician Duke Ellington and his rise to fame after experiencing career failure. In the 1930s and '40s, with hits like "Take the A Train" and "Mood Indigo," Ellington had the most popular big band in America. In 1955, as Goldsmith writes, he was "reduced to accompanying ice skaters at a rink in Long Island." In the summer of 1956, things weren't looking so good for Ellington's late-night performance at the Newport Jazz Festival. Band members didn't show up, the crowd was leaving, and he had waited three hours to perform. Then something crazy happened. Determined to put on a great show, Ellington asked his saxophonist, Paul Gonsalves, to play a big solo, and the virtuoso launched into a furious performance. Magic happened. The crowd filed back into their seats, and soon people were dancing in the aisles. The next day, newspapers all over the world announced, "Ellington Is Back!" and the following month he was on the cover of *TIME* magazine. He later celebrated his seventieth birthday at the White House. What a comeback story![6]

Here's the lesson: Failure is not final. It's the start of a new story.

There's another way to snatch good news out of bad, and that's not to allow your emotions to rule the day. I had a client, Paul, who was *extremely* angry. For thirty years, he had given his all to the company where he worked. Weekends, holidays, overtime, he had done whatever it took to get the job done, satisfy the client, and generate considerable revenue for his employer. The announcement floored him—a major corporate downsizing and just like that, he was out of a job. He had poured his heart and soul into this company and now he was angry and bitter.

Paul had a decision to make. Over the years, he had accumulated quite a bit of company stock, and in his anger, his first instinct was to sell it all. I counseled Paul and his wife to take some breaths, that while I understood their emotions, they now needed to think like savvy investors and not allow a personal crisis to become a financial one. I told them that while I understood their sour feelings, the outlook for the company looked positive and the stock was still a good investment. Reluctantly, they agreed, and during the next two years, the company's stock doubled. Paul and his wife profited by several hundred thousand dollars. Despite their anger, they were self-aware enough not to allow their emotions to rule their financial decision-making. That's what you call taking a bunch of lemons and turning them into some delicious lemonade.

CHAPTER 16

Rise and Shine or Rise and Whine

WHEN KARA AND I were first married, we were part of a church small group that met regularly. All the couples were of similar ages and life experiences. It was a place where you could be yourself. In our times together, each couple shared what was going on in their lives, and we aimed to encourage one another in the ups and downs of day-to-day living. Life wasn't perfect for any of us, but we kept moving forward and gained comfort from the feeling that we were all in this together.

There was one couple in the group, however, who always seemed to have a dark cloud hanging over their heads. Their voices were tired; a feeling of hopelessness was consistently tied to their words. They would repeat the same sentiment during every meeting: "Once we get through this, *then* we'll be okay. Once *this* is over, *then* we can relax."

I often think of that couple and the lessons they taught me. They lived their lives believing that only *after* whatever problem or issue they were facing had passed would they experience peace and joy.

Here's the truth: that rarely happens. Life is filled with adversity and mistakes. Jon Gordon has a similar message. "We can't go back and focus on what we've lost," he told me. "We have to look forward. You can either become *more* during this time [of adversity], or you can become *less*, and really, we have to work on becoming *more*. You can rise and shine each day or rise and whine."[1] It's your choice.

When I started my career as an investment advisor, I knew it would mean intensive study for a lot of different licensing requirements, and that I would have to drum up business, but I didn't anticipate the amount of rejection I would face. I naively thought I'd pick up the phone and people would say, "I've been waiting all my life for you." But mostly, I didn't even get rejection. They didn't even say no. They didn't waste their breath; it was just *click, click, click.* I learned that as long as you can embrace rejection, become accustomed to it, and actually learn to like it as part of the process, you're going to do great. I know plenty of people in the same business—really bright finance people from major companies—who on paper should have done very, very well, but who washed out quickly because they didn't have sufficiently thick skin to keep pushing through their emotions.

Even after building a successful business, my professional heartaches didn't stop there. About fifteen years ago, I targeted my first acquisition, a group of financial planning firms in Dallas. I had done a lot of research and was convinced it was a good opportunity for me. The systems and structure I had put in place for our business had delivered significant value to my other clients and helped them do well financially, and I knew I could do this for my new clients in Dallas. One of my banker friends went so far as to say that even if I had to pull money out of my retirement account for the down payment, then "Do it, Derrick!"

The moment the deal closed, however, all hell broke loose. The advisors at the firms I acquired had all signed non-compete agreements, as was standard with these kinds of deals, but they used what they thought was a loophole to begin trying to steal back their clients, who were the key to what I had purchased. They even began spreading rumors about me. I began losing money fast, and the loans I had taken out to acquire the company were coming due.

A mentor taught me many years ago that most things in life can be placed into one of three buckets:

1. What I can control.
2. What I can influence.
3. What I can neither control nor influence.

He told me that the best use of my time was to focus on Bucket #1.

There's a long list of things I can't control—what happens in the world, the weather, how someone might respond if I accidentally cut them off in traffic. I can only control myself. I couldn't change what had happened to me, but I could *choose* my next move. Would I retreat or would I lean in and advance ahead? I remember for a fleeting moment considering bankruptcy, but as Kara and I talked, she reminded me that when I faced adversity, I always worked my way through it. In that moment, my personal fire was relit. I quickly learned that even with all the fancy, supposedly airtight legal agreements in place, an agreement was really only as good as the people who signed it. If a person chooses to violate it, the damage is done.

You never really win a legal issue with a personal services company; you try to stop the hemorrhaging. The damage was done, so I decided to take action. I called my attorney. I moved my office across the highway. The legal battle cost me a lot of money and even more emotional energy, but I came to realize that sometimes you pay to buy a business, and sometimes you pay extra for the lessons buying that business can teach you. I paid both.

In the face of adversity, not only did my business grow, but perhaps even more importantly, *I* grew. I learned the value of betting on myself, and that was a skill I would utilize again many more times—most recently when I sold my investment advisory business to launch Good Money Framework.

A friend once told me about a gymnastics coach he had as a child who told him, "Put your head down and proceed confidently and your torso and legs will follow right behind." In other words, where your head goes, your body will follow, or "behavior follows belief."

In a sense, that's how I've always behaved when it comes to money—I act out of the beliefs that I create. Let me explain.

As a financial advisor, I've helped thousands of people invest well and achieve their life-long financial goals. As a result, I've developed a strong belief that I'm good with money, so when I face setbacks, whether an investment choice or a business decision that went south, I take a breath to assess. What led me to make that particular decision? What can I learn from it? What will I do differently next time? Then I wipe my mental whiteboard clean and choose not to wallow in what happened in the past. Instead, I choose to recognize the courage I showed by making the decision in the first place. I took action, and now I move forward without recrimination. You can too.

Andy Andrews, the author of several books, including *The Seven Decisions* and *The Bottom of the Pool*, told me, "It's critical to note that we can't gather enough information to make right decisions all the time, but we can gather enough information to *make* a decision and then go about the process of making it work. You can't leave home every day and guarantee that you're not gonna run into a detour, but when you run into a detour on your way to the office, you don't just start crying and go, 'Oh, I'll never drive a car again! I didn't know it was gonna be like this.' But people do that with their lives."[2]

Once you know the *when*, it's just a matter of the *how*. When you decide to do something and the outcome is clear, then it's just performing the steps to reach your goal. When you begin to anticipate that problems will inevitably occur, your life becomes dramatically better. I've heard from psychologists that the average person experiences three to four crises each year, interrupted by the occasional emergency. That means on average, you're either heading into a crisis or coming out of one. That's what we call life, folks. The struggle is real; embrace it.

I don't think I realized until after my dad passed how much his hopes and dreams for me impacted my drive for success. He was never very successful financially, but I can still hear him telling my sister and me, "Nothing ventured, nothing gained." I don't think it's unrelated that my favorite quote is from Teddy Roosevelt:

> It is not the critic who counts; not the man who points out how the strong man stumbles or where the doer of deeds could have done them better. The credit belongs to the man who is actually in the arena, whose face is marred by dust and sweat and blood; who strives valiantly; who errs, who comes short again and again, because there is no effort without error and shortcoming; but who does actually strive to do the deeds; who knows the great enthusiasms, the great devotions; who spends himself in a worthy cause; who at the best knows in the end the triumph of high achievement, and who at the worst, if he fails, at least fails while daring greatly, so that his

place shall never be with those cold and timid souls
who neither know victory nor defeat.[3]

Independence is a core value of mine. Kara and I have raised
four very independent children. They're not needy, which has its
downsides, but we don't feel like we have to rescue them all the
time. It also leads to them knowing we believe in their abilities to
make good decisions.

I've taken the lessons I've learned as an investment advisor
and used them in how I try to rear my children. Or maybe it's
that I've taken the lessons I've learned from my children and used
them in how I run my business. Either way, I know that when
advising people about their long-term investments, I like to help
them become more independent, to live out their stories. Even if
the process is sprinkled with failure and feelings of hopelessness,
I've seen people overcome huge money mistakes and failures and
open a fresh page. Sometimes they may need help turning a page
or putting words on paper, but it's *their* story, and they deserve to
live it fully. The same is true for you.

CHAPTER 17

Sweet Spot Solution: The Ultimate Retirement Redemption Plan

*By failing to prepare,
you are preparing to fail.* —Benjamin Franklin

*Give me six hours to chop down a tree and I will spend
the first four sharpening the axe.* —Abraham Lincoln

*It takes as much energy to wish
as it does to plan.* —Eleanor Roosevelt

*If you don't know where you are going,
you'll end up someplace else.* —Yogi Berra

It's time to get busy living or get busy dying.
—Andy to Red in the movie *The Shawshank Redemption*

OKAY, I DIDN'T interview any of these people, either for my podcast *or* this book, but they all knew something I've been saying on repeat for years: live life with intention. Most people cringe when told the importance of planning, but just like planning a vacation, if you don't plan for your retirement, it's going to arrive and you're not going to have a clue. You plan for your vacations because you know that otherwise you may not be able to travel at the best time or to the most desired location. You may not be able to get airline reservations or get into a great hotel. If you leave it all to chance, the odds are stacked against you and your dream vacation might never get off the ground. Even if you get there, you may have to settle for whatever is left, which doesn't always sound so good. Here's the scary truth: People spend more time planning their next vacation than they do planning their retirement.

Retirement doesn't have to be scary. In fact, planning for it can be exciting and fun. Learning about all your options, finding special places to go, and creating enjoyable experiences—there's a lot to look forward to.

Many of you may feel like you're behind in your retirement savings or don't have a clear course of action. You're worried it's too late to start saving and planning. After all, you didn't see your parents model a fun and relaxing retirement. I have some good news for you! It's called the "Sweet Spot Solution." It's that wonderful window when your children are no longer financially dependent, when they've finished school and are on their own, you're closing in on paying off your house, and you have discretionary savings available. For some of you, that may be five to fifteen years when you can "catch up." The key is to capture it and make up for lost time. Finally, after spending so much on your children, the time has come for you to make up for lost ground and build for your own future. Now it is time to think about how you wish to live when you retire, address your finances, and begin to fulfill your dreams.

In a nutshell, the Sweet Spot Solution follows the same approach you would take to plan a dream vacation. First, decide *where* you want to go, then *when*, then *how* you wish to travel, and *how long* you plan to stay. Locate your options, determine how much each will cost, and make your decisions. Then figure out how to finance it.

After a lifetime of working, most baby boomers don't want their parents' version of retirement. They don't want to slip away quietly, hibernate, or follow traditional routes. They want to pursue their passions, explore, experience, and blaze new trails. They insist on controlling their own destinies and setting their own standards, as they always have. You may not want to completely give up your job, what you've mastered over a lifetime, been praised for, and come to love. You may want to continue working, perhaps part-time, or even start a new career you've been dreaming about. Or maybe you want to travel, play golf, fish, volunteer, or just relax. And, after a few years, you may even itch for something different.

Regardless of the choices you make, don't kid yourself—they all revolve around money. When I met with clients for the first time, very few had thought much about their retirement, and fewer still had made any specific plans. Instead, they had been grinding it out, living for today, and postponing the inevitable. When we talked about creating investment plans, they didn't want to change their lifestyle now or later, so they cringed—and resisted.

The Sweet Spot Solution gives you the opportunity to:

1. Retire now with a lower standard of living (this is for the person who desperately wants out of their job).
2. Phase in your retirement so you work longer and begin to ease into retirement while doing work you enjoy.
3. Delay full retirement—work full-time longer so that when you do retire, you won't have to work at all.

Planning for retirement is essential, so don't be afraid of it. The Sweet Spot Solution starts with six steps. It teaches those who haven't saved or haven't saved enough how to plan for retirement, build retirement funds, and address the emotional impact of the changes they'll face. It shows those who have saved how to save more and surpass their dreams. And it will arm you with time-tested answers to problems that could throw you off course, show you how to anticipate these issues, and give you concrete ways to proactively create a worry-free retirement.

- **Step one: Take a financial X-ray.** Identify where you presently stand financially. What is your net worth, your income, expenses, and current monthly savings? This is your starting point. It's a reality check, so be brutally honest and don't fudge the numbers. You'll have to overcome financial fear with financial courage. Usually, your situation isn't as formidable as you had feared. Examine each of your worries and decide how they should be approached.
- **Step two: Review your money in motion.** Trace the movement of your money. You may be surprised at how much you're throwing away. How much are you spending and on what? Find out how much you're saving, how much you're investing, and what you're getting in return.
- **Step three: Assess your asset protection plan.** How well are you protected? What type of life, disability, long-term care, umbrella liability, auto insurance, and home insurance do you have? Is each the proper amount? Are you paying too much?
- **Step four: Envision your retirement.** At what age would you like to be financially independent, having enough money to retire? How much would you like to live on? Where do you want to live, and how would you prefer to spend your time? Think about the answers that make sense for *you*. Choose the lifestyle *you* want, how *you* would like to live in retirement. Do you want to sit on the back porch and watch the grass grow, or would you rather keep working at least part-time, volunteer, or travel? Identify your personal goals and dreams.

- **Step five: Determine your spendable monthly income goal.** If you were to retire today, how much money would you need to live on? How much would you like to spend each month on the things you want? How committed are you to paying off your debt? Be realistic.
- **Step six: The Sweet Spot commitment.** How much are you willing to save each month or each year in order to catch up and make your financial dreams a reality? What are you willing to give up or change in your life so that you have more, save more, and give more?

The Sweet Spot Solution is based on the fact that we all have unique circumstances, goals, and objectives. It enables you to create an individualized plan with realistic steps, time frames, and outcomes, instead of trying to fit into stock formulas that may not be right for you. To ensure you make the best decisions possible, make certain you make all your decisions jointly with your spouse or significant other and your financial advisor. Discuss how you can economize without drastically changing your life—how to be more efficient, to free up money, to save and invest. Then work on changing your outlook by changing your attitude. Retirement planning can actually be a positive, enjoyable experience—even exciting, rewarding, and fun. If you're dreading your retirement rather than looking forward to it, it's time to think differently. As I worked with my clients, their enthusiasm grew. Their dread often turned into excitement. Before long, they became more positive and more involved. They got fully on board. When they felt that a plan had been personalized for them, they worked harder to reach their goals.

Don't be afraid to fail and try new things. When I met with Tony and Latosha, they were convinced they wanted to sell their house, buy an RV, and tour this great country. I asked them,

"Have you ever driven an RV?" They said no. I suggested that before they bought one, they rent one for a weekend. "Kick the tires a bit—a low-cost probe to test if you're prepared for all that comes with RV ownership." They took my advice, and while they enjoyed their weekend, they decided they didn't want to own an RV after all. Their decision saved them tens of thousands of dollars. The lesson is this: try it and test it. You can always readjust your course.

Working with my clients taught me that people will work for what they want, but when they don't know what they want, it's impossible to do the work. My approach showed them the way and taught them how to get what they wanted.

Here's the real secret sauce: boldness, courage, and monitoring your progress. These three pull the six steps together. Two or three times per year, evaluate your progress. Life happens. Sometimes it can knock you off course.

In 1877, the USS *Huron* set sail from New York. At the time, it was called the Navy's best ship. It was state of the art and deemed a perfect vessel. The ship drifted off course in heavy seas and a bad storm caused a shipwreck. A small compass error was largely to blame. It led them to drift off course and subsequently hit a reef off the coast of the Carolinas.[1]

The last thing I want for you is to feel like you're a passenger on the USS *Huron*. You have the chance to create the retirement of your dreams, even if today is the first time you've started thinking about it. One small shift in your life can change your course forever.

The choices you make today have a tremendous impact on your financial future. You have the power to make the difference you want, when and where you want to make it. Use the Sweet Spot Solution to help you get there.

CHAPTER 18

The Seven Biggest Retirement Mistakes You Can Make

UNFORTUNATELY, SOME OF you are experiencing the precise opposite of the Sweet Spot Solution. For many people approaching retirement age, particularly baby boomers, their plans for the next stage of their life have hit a roadblock they never anticipated. Suddenly they realize they are not on their own after all. They're providing emotional and financial support for their aging parents (and maybe their kids living in the basement), and their retirement dreams seem to be fading further and further into the future. It's the perfect storm.

Even after the best-laid plans are put into place, surprises will jump out at you. Just as you are about to leap into the new adventure you've been dreaming about for years, suddenly Mom or Dad needs your help, your son or daughter hits a rough patch, and you have to put your own plans on hold.

Life is expensive. Raising a family costs a bundle. Tuition, healthcare, and insurance costs are exorbitant, and the prices of food, oil, and gas have gone through the roof. (And the roof probably needs replacing.) That's not even counting the endless outflow for all the cool clothing, sports equipment, and electronics every kid seems to need. Most parents are so involved in supporting their families and making ends meet that they find it difficult, if not impossible, to save for retirement. And it never gets easier.

Retirement seems so distant, daunting, and complex. Planning means dealing with lawyers, accountants, insurance agents, and financial advisors, which is neither fun nor free. Most people are intimidated and don't know where to start, so they concentrate on the immediate—getting through their busy lives and allowing time to pass without any serious planning—forgetting that the future is not that far off. In 2019, of the 71.6 million baby boomers,[1] 45 percent had no retirement savings and only 20 percent had set aside $500,000 or more.[2] They don't know where to turn, so they do nothing, allowing the problem to magnify. Or they make costly mistakes and exacerbate the situation.

You've worked for thirty, forty, or fifty years and suddenly now you're faced with, "What am I retiring to?" It's like a blank piece of paper, which, for some people, can make them feel very, very nervous; they don't want to make mistakes. At least when they're earning a salary, if they blow the paycheck, there's another one coming right behind it. In retirement, if you make a few irrevocably wrong decisions, it could cost you the retirement you've worked all those years to achieve.

One of the questions I am frequently asked is, "How much money do I need to retire?" You need to find out for yourself.

When Jim and Ellen came to see me, they were beyond frustrated. One book they read told them that in order to retire comfortably, they'd need to live on 80 percent of their pre-retirement salary. Then a talking head on television announced they should have 90 percent of their pre-retirement salary because in today's world, people tend to spend *more* money after they stop working. Then the following week, good friends who had already retired told them they lived comfortably on only half of what they had while they were working. Exasperated, Jim and Ellen paid me a visit. Their first question was the most obvious one: "Derrick, how much income do we need to have in retirement?"

I gave them some simple, but perhaps not so obvious, advice. I recommended that they live on a "practice retirement budget" for three months. I told them what they already knew; there are many different guidelines suggested by the experts. But I also told them the reason there was such widespread disagreement was that money, particularly how you spend it, is personal. How you choose to spend it is solely up to you, but there is one common denominator. For your plan to be effective, and for you to believe it will be effective, it has to be tailored for you and you alone.

I suggested to Jim and Ellen that for the next ninety days, they keep a log of all they spent, after which we'd review their experience, and together, we'd fine-tune their strategy. They were excited about the idea and highly motivated. To be certain they strictly abided by their monthly spending goals, they direct-deposited their current paychecks into a new, separate account that we set up and asked me each month to send them the amount they thought they'd need in retirement. They wanted to leave nothing to chance to verify what would be necessary when their "practice retirement" became real.

After the first month, we made some adjustments, but once the three months had passed, they had nailed it. They reported how liberating it was to know they could actually retire earlier than they thought because they had tested precisely the amount they'd need. The beauty of this strategy was that they did all this while they were still working. All it took was the time and focus to track what they were spending and to test it before making major life decisions.

This will work for you too. A year or two before retirement, take a test drive to see if you'll be able to live on the amount of money you've allocated. Your first step will be to develop a practice budget to identify your current expenses and those that will diminish during retirement, as well as those that may increase. Then determine how much you'll need for your monthly living expenses. Use a spreadsheet to track your progress. If you can live within your retirement budget, it will give you confidence because you may even find you have more wiggle room than you thought. Maybe you really can take that long-delayed trip to Hawaii.

For some, this process might be a wake-up call; for others, it will confirm what they thought they were spending and what they'll need. But regardless, the three months don't lie; the numbers reveal the truth. For Jim and Ellen, it gave them the peace of mind that they could retire earlier than they had anticipated. For others, it might mean delaying retirement for a year or two while savings and monthly Social Security benefits increase.

I want to remove any doubt you have that this can work for you. Like using an eraser on a whiteboard, remove that old money mentality and let me help you create your ideal retirement scenario so you know you're retiring to something fabulous and that you're not going to run out of money.

Now I'm going to walk you through each of the seven worst retirement mistakes people make and tell you exactly how to avoid them.

1. Not calculating your magic number.

The magic number is the amount of money you need so you can retire and not worry about running out of money. Is it $500,000, a million dollars, or $250,000? Whatever that number is, it's going to be based on your specific situation, including the income you'll be getting from Social Security or a pension. No one can tell you, "Here's what you need." Some people say you need 90 percent of your pre-retirement income. Some people say 75 percent or 60 percent. All those numbers mean nothing because all that matters is how it impacts you and your personal economy.

On a sheet of paper or in the notes app on your phone, list your retirement income on the left side. This will include Social Security, a company pension, and any other money you will be receiving in retirement that is consistent every month. Maybe you have rental property income; include that too. Some income, like any sort of royalties, may have to be estimated.

On the right side, list your investments, totaling how much you have in cash, stocks, in accounts such as your 401(k) or IRA, and any other savings.

Once you've used your practice retirement budget to determine how much you'll need each month, take your income and your fixed income and calculate the gap. Assume a monthly withdrawal of 2 to 3 percent from your portfolio. Some people used to suggest 4 percent, but with inflation creeping up, it's best to be conservative. As I like to say, plan conservatively but invest aggressively. That way you're more likely not to run out of money in retirement.

2. Not setting financial goals for yourself.

So many people I speak with say, "Derrick, if I can just make it to Friday, or if I can just make it through this year, if I can just retire, then my life will be better."

Marty was tired. He shared with me how he felt trapped in a dead-end job. While his steady sales position gave him the opportunity to earn more, it seemed like life emergencies always had their hands out first. "Derrick, I don't feel like I have goals. I don't know where I'm going." Marty was working fifty to sixty hours a week, and when he got home, the last thing he wanted to worry about was how he was going to finance his retirement. I suggested he write down the answers to three simple questions related to his financial goals:

- When do you want to retire?
- How much money do you want to have in retirement?
- When you close your eyes, what does life in retirement look like to you?

"Put the answers on a sticky note," I told him, "and place it on your mirror, by your nightstand, in the kitchen, or on your car dashboard."

Your goal is to stay focused in your busy life with its many distractions. If you're not looking at your goals on a regular basis, you can easily get so far off target that you can't make it back in time. So take some time now to write down three financial goals important to you. Look at them every day, and you're going to be far more likely to make progress toward what you really want.

3. Not creating a plan to reach your retirement goals.

This one causes so many people not to have the retirement they've always wanted. I don't think people plan to fail; they simply fail to plan. Take a weekend with your spouse or significant other and just talk through what is it that you want to do in retirement. Make sure you're on the same page and write down those three things. I like to think in terms of three because it's easy to remember, easy to implement, and easy to keep you on track. Every quarter, sit down again and monitor your progress. If you do that, you're much more likely to achieve your goals and not wake up one day wondering what the heck happened.

4. Not investing to create income.

Think about this. If you were going to climb a mountain, your strategy to climb up the mountain would be vastly different than the strategy for getting back down. We call climbing the mountain *accumulation*. We call the descent down the mountain *distribution*. Accumulating money and taking money out of your investments are two completely different strategies. So while you can invest in a variety of tools that defer taxes, which allows your money to grow more quickly while you're working, the goal in retirement is to generate conservative, predictable income. You'll want to work with an advisor skilled in income maximization strategies—how to position your money so that it generates income. That might be in the form of annuities or in other vehicles that generate income you can pull out each year.

Real estate, high-dividend exchange-traded funds, and preferred stocks are also considerations. All these may come together to generate an income strategy. Remember, your income subtracted from the amount you'll need in retirement is the gap that you will need to generate. And keep in mind (I say this jokingly), the government will never give you a loan for your retirement. It's completely up to you. So begin now to practice living on the income you'll actually need.

5. Not setting up an automatic savings plan.

Money has been made so complicated that it causes people to take no action at all. We want to keep money simple. Put the maximum allowable into your company's 401(k) plan. If you're self-employed, it's called a SEP. Whatever the acronym of your retirement account, the bottom line is that the government incentivizes you to save for retirement. Make sure you're taking advantage of these opportunities. If you work for a company, oftentimes they will match a portion of what you put in. Never pass up free money. Make sure your contributions automatically come out of your paycheck, or if you're self-employed, set it up so it comes out of your bank account on the first or fifteenth of each month.

6. Not being on the same page about money as your spouse.

Tara and Keith had been married for twenty-seven years. Tara worked full-time in the home managing the house and the children, while Keith was a consultant for a marketing firm who traveled weekly, Tuesdays to Fridays. As we began to plan and talk through what they really wanted to do in retirement, Keith said that because he'd been on the road so long, he wanted to stay at home and watch the grass grow and just relax. His wife, however, because she was home all the time, wanted to do things and see the world. As you can imagine, that created conflict.

The challenge was how to get them on the same page. We talked about a seasonal approach. "How about this?" I asked them. "What if you decided you would take a couple trips a year together, and other trips with friends?" They thought about that and decided it would give them both exactly what they wanted. They both got to travel, they both got to rest. They got time together and time apart.

Don't be surprised when you retire after a busy working life and suddenly you're getting to know your spouse all over again. The darker side of that coin is that I've seen a few couples divorce once they realized the activity and urgency of daily living had blurred the fact that they had grown so far apart. They weren't even aware how far they had drifted. I encourage you to talk with your significant other well in advance of retirement to get on the same page, and for each of you to get excited about what you're going to be retiring to, and not just from. That's one of the biggest keys to planning for a successful retirement.

7. Not purchasing long-term care insurance.

Long-term care insurance is this non-sexy part of retirement planning, but picture this: Mom or Dad, while they may be in good health now, might need care in the future that you simply can't provide. The issue is twofold. First, I like to call this "asset protection insurance." A long-term care facility can cost many thousands of dollars per month, much of which will have to come right out of their portfolio. A better and more cost-effective way to handle this is to have an insurance company partially offset that risk. This has to be done while your mom or dad are in good health, and that goes for you too.

The key is to determine how much risk you want to keep and how much you want to give away. Some people I've helped wanted to protect their entire portfolio, so they purchased a more extensive type of plan that would pay for almost everything. Other people decided that the odds of using this type of coverage were low, so they decided to cover a portion of the risk and consequently paid a lower premium.

These decisions are very personal. You'll want to have a serious family meeting to review everyone's particular circumstances. One son or daughter may be home full-time and may be able to become a caregiver to a parent, while another child might be in a position to be more of a financial caregiver. As long as there's open communication between children and parents, you'll get through it by making the best decisions for everyone. In any scenario, however, some level of long-term care insurance is likely appropriate.

Smart decisions combined with savvy saving lead to success. These seven retirement mistakes will cost you money and time—two things you need more of. I want to help you live the life you've always imagined—and that starts with wisely planning for the future and making sure you're taking the steps to do what you want, when you want to do it.

CHAPTER 19

Your Biggest Retirement Questions Answered

RETIREMENT CAN BE a scary word. Over the years, I have answered many questions from clients, television viewers, and podcast listeners. I'm here to guide you through this unique transition in your life, whether it's now or in a few years. You probably have some of the same questions, so let's dive in.

First, let's talk about the fear of running out of money. You're likely going to worry when you see global events occur, financial crises, inflation, stock market volatility, and the value of your investments dropping. But once you begin to embrace the fact that these are worries you'll likely have for the rest of your life, they will become more palatable as concerns. What you want to do, though, is to plan conservatively.

Many years ago, I had a seventy-five-year-old client come into the office who said to me, "Derrick, I only want to earn about a 15 percent return. I want to be really conservative." Well, keep in mind, this was 1999, the market was red, red hot, and everybody was making money. She thought, *How hard could this be?* What you don't want to do—and this is a surefire way to make retirement *not* what you want—is to take out all of the gains you make on your account for your income. Let's say one year, you're up 20 percent, the next year, you're down 15 percent. You quickly learn the lesson not to base your lifestyle on what you can't control—it's a shaky foundation. If you're withdrawing only 2 to 3 percent per year on average from your retirement account, you should be okay.

Here's what I would tell you: Many people want to take a big trip each year—a cruise, travel across the country to see their grandkids, or overseas. When your investments go up, talk to your advisor about locking in some of those gains, capturing that money, and putting it into a conservative account. That way, you've paid for your cruise already. It's frustrating when you know you could have locked-in profits, but then the market drops all the way back down again and you've lost that opportunity. Let the market pay for some of what you want to do in retirement and be strategic about it.

The next popular question is about ways to save money during retirement. When you think about saving, you want to look at required versus optional expenses. So many people think that their expenses will drop precipitously when they retire, but they typically don't.

Maybe you'll spend less on dry cleaning, but you may offset that with more on gas, traveling, eating out, and enjoying an active lifestyle. Think about some expenses you can cut, but do it from a purpose-driven standpoint. For example, if you're going to cut the number of cable channels you pay for, make sure it doesn't include your favorite channels. You can have some small luxuries on the cheap and not have to cut everything all the way down to the quick, if you will. Or if you love having someone clean your house, keep that expense but offset it somewhere else. You don't have to live like a pauper in retirement. The goal is to live the lifestyle you want and that you've always enjoyed, but to be prudent about how you choose to spend your money.

Once you've figured out how to save for retirement, it is easy to question if it's actually enough. This leads me to my third most frequently asked question: How can I boost my retirement income? The key here comes down to risk. Most very conservative income-producing investments are that way because there's very little risk. Think, for example, about large blue chip dividend-paying companies. While their stock prices do fluctuate, they're unlikely to go out of business. Another good strategy is to work with your advisor and take advantage of what's called dollar cost averaging, which simply means easing very gradually into a certain investment. That gives you some growth potential, some "pop" if you will, while still minimizing the risk that you will mistime market fluctuations.

Now, here's an emotional question that many people struggle with: "What if my parents really need to start thinking about retirement, but every time I've talked to them about it they don't seem interested? What should I do?"

This is a common concern, but keep in mind, you want to approach this issue with grace and empathy. A good way to begin the conversation is to say something like, "You know, Mom and Dad, I've been doing some thinking and some reading on people who have a successful retirement. Would you mind if I asked you a question?" So you ask permission from them to start a dialogue. They will likely agree, even if grudgingly, and then you can say, "If you don't mind me asking, what does your retirement look like? What do you have planned? What are some of your thoughts?" The goal is simply to open the door for discussion.

Don't make the fatal mistake of trying to solve the entire retirement question in one conversation. That will just lead to a blowup and nobody talking at all. Instead, you want to open the door to just see where it goes and then gently close the door until next time. Now you've established some trust, and they don't feel like you're questioning every decision they've made. Instead, you're walking alongside them, which is a much better way of working together to achieve a common goal.

At the start of a road trip, you start your car, begin moving, and make adjustments as you go. While in the driveway, you can't anticipate every traffic outcome, like if you'll have a blowout or if there will be a sudden change in the weather. The same is true with retirement. You might have to bounce back after adversity and make adjustments along the way. Expect mistakes—believe me, you will make them. But no matter how old you are, you now know the biggest retirement mistakes people make and how to achieve the retirement you've always wanted.

What happens when it feels like you just can't get out from under your past money mistakes and that paralyzing fear of failure? In Part 2, we'll explore the different money mindsets you're going to encounter and how to conquer each of them to build lasting wealth and impact for you and your family.

PART 2
Bad Money

CHAPTER 20

Is Your Money Mindset Holding You Back?

MONEY IS *GOOD* and you should have more of it.

Sounds simple enough, right? It is simple—but that doesn't mean the rest of the world agrees. For many people money has been villainized, most likely because they've grown up believing money is bad and that people who have it are bad. Choosing to continue on this revolutionary Good Money journey is going to require a completely new perspective. In order for you to start making more money so you can give more away, you will have to overcome any negative money mindsets that hold you back from living the life of impact you desire. In this section, we're going to pinpoint exactly where these beliefs are rooted and how to push back against them so you can make more money and remake the world.

Let's say you grew up believing money is bad. You've seen it cause division and hopelessness in your family. At work, the highest paid people are the most arrogant. The wealthy are selfish and spoiled. If that is what having money does to a person, you're not interested. Besides, the thought of making and managing money feels complicated, time-consuming, and a hassle.

You feel your anxiety rising and your motivation dropping whenever you even think about making more money. Sound familiar?

Picture yourself as a child at the dinner table having a meal with your family. What did that look like? Did it consist of arguments about not having enough money? Was there a fist that suddenly banged on the table with an accompanying voice saying, "If we only had more money," we could do this or that? If money wasn't working *for* us, it was working *against* us, and in that case, we're not going to have the life we've always wanted. Money was the enemy.

"I think for people like that, it's really worthwhile to take some time out and just unpack your history with money," says Bola Sokunbi. "Unpack your first memories with money. . . . Look at what was surrounding that memory, what was surrounding that situation. What were the causes of that positive memory or that negative memory?" Bola reminds us that we, ultimately, are in control and suggests replicating the positive experiences and throwing the negative ones under the bus. "Money is simply a tool. It doesn't have emotions. It doesn't have feelings. It does what you tell it."[1]

Bola agrees that the cultural vibe that money is bad may well hearken back to a person's childhood. As we get older, that feeling becomes transformed into the idea that, "If I can't have it, you can't have it either." According to Rabbi Daniel Lapin, "Generally speaking, people tend to feel that money is grubby, money is of this world, money implies that you don't really care about spiritual matters and the higher realms of things."[2] He adds, "There's no question in my mind that a good deal of money shortage comes from this deeply implanted idea that 'I better not have too much of it because that would signal to people that I must be a pretty bad person.'"[3]

When we think about money as being bad, oftentimes we villainize those who have a lot of it. I understand that for many people, the issue is one of fairness. Is it right that Jeff Bezos's net worth topped $200 billion in 2020 while millions of Americans were struggling to feed their families?[4] Is it right for one person to have so much money?

I know this is a very hot topic for many of you—and I'm not here to tell you the answer or take a side. But I *do* want to offer you something to consider. Think about Jeff Bezos, Elon Musk, or any other member of the gazillionaire club. Some of them had their net worth double during the pandemic, so it's no surprise they are not immune to criticism. At the same time, many people have lost their livelihoods and taken a serious hit financially. The most common response? Choosing to yell, scream, and accuse the wealthy while saying, "Look, you have too much money. You need to share it with the rest of us."

That's one option, but here's how I see it. These people had an idea, took a risk, experienced multiple failures and disappointments, and through tenacity and grit built a valuable brand. It's not as if entrepreneurs were born with a business already built for them (not most of them, at any rate). At the time of his birth, Jeff Bezos's mother was a seventeen-year-old high school student, and his biological father only stuck around for the first months of Bezos's life.[5] I'd be willing to bet that when Bezos first had the idea of an online bookstore, people weren't picketing his home office. Flash forward to today, and we see a high level of vitriol, and even disdain, for Bezos and wealthy entrepreneurs like him. But the source of their wealth is commonly misunderstood.

When you start a company, you usually own lots of stock. As the founder, a significant portion of your net worth is tied to your company's stock. If the stock price goes down, you lose money. If the stock price goes up, your net worth grows sharply.

Let me give you an example. The pandemic occurred and people began shopping online in droves. One of the biggest beneficiaries of that was Amazon. Online sales set record numbers, which led to a burgeoning stock price. If a person has tons of Amazon stock and the stock price grows sharply, what happens? A dramatic increase in wealth.

That's exactly what Jeff Bezos experienced.

1. His net worth grew during the pandemic primarily because of how well Amazon's stock price did because more people used and benefited from the convenience his company offered. I know I did.
2. If you owned Amazon stock during COVID, you likely made money. I did.
3. If you followed the trends of the COVID economy, you saw people purchase Peloton bikes to exercise at home, spend hours a week on Zoom calls, and order Chipotle food delivery every week.

The result? Those stocks performed well. Did you own them? I did. While all these companies might have benefited your life, here's the common yet ironic response: "Shame on you for having a valuable service that many people needed during the pandemic and making a ton of money doing it."

MacKenzie Scott, who received a 4 percent stake in Amazon (valued at tens of billions and continuing to grow) when she and Jeff Bezos divorced, is donating massive amounts of money to causes she believes in.[6] I read plenty of comments on Twitter claiming Scott should donate more because her donations were merely the tip of the iceberg compared to her vast wealth. But do you think the organizations should send back the money because it's not enough for *them*?

I don't have a lot of excess breath or brain cells to spend criticizing people who are working hard to make money. But if they are oppressing others, withholding fair opportunities, or any other issues of malfeasance, then that's not right, and it needs to be addressed. If you are saying a person is bad because they own a company from which millions of people derive great value—including you—don't count on me to join you as you lob criticisms.

Here's what I know for sure: Becoming financially successful takes risk. It requires stepping out into the unknown, pursuing one's goal without knowing whether it will work or not, and having the desire, initiative, and the stick-to-itiveness to keep at it. The reward that follows the risk is not guaranteed. Yet money and wealth are not in limited supply. Remember, money is like a river: it flows where value is received.

My point is this: Go make money. And position your money wisely so when future opportunities arise, you can make even more of it to do more good.

I challenge you to press pause, reset, and ask yourself, "What are the ideas that successful entrepreneurs have conceptualized that I can begin to imitate, even in a small way?" Could you become the next business titan? You won't hear from me not to try. Expect the naysayers—that's just part of the deal. Most world changers aren't without cynics.

Philanthropist Tom Golisano told me he's come to accept criticisms of his status as a billionaire and knows that his work is helping to make his community better. "If you create a company, and it's profitable, and as a byproduct you create jobs, you create fringe benefits for employees, you create real estate values—you do all those things when you have a profitable enterprise. If there are a few people that think it's bad, too bad on them. But for the community, nothing works better than having profitable organizations in the community to create jobs and to create charitable contributions."[7]

John O'Leary agrees. "Those who have assets frequently are chastised for having assets, when frequently those doing the chastising forget the fact that those who have received have worked very diligently, very intentionally, to obtain those. But they're also forgetting the fact that they've created wealth for others: employees, shareholders, communities. They've been charitable, generous, and they're trying to mentor the next generation. They're not trying to shrink the pie. . . . They're actually trying to expand it. They believe in the law of abundance. And so I think it's really important we recognize good money can do good things in the community in the hands of good people."[8]

Continue to criticize the wealthy or start putting yourself on a path to creating wealth. Both take time. You can waste it, or you can invest it by learning the principles that help create success and then apply them to your situation.

The question is not what the wealthy have done; the question is what you are going to do. Let's face it. There are bad people out there, and some of them have a lot of money, which likely means they're doing bad things with their money. You've probably figured this out, and it may bother you. It bothers me too. But let's step back and look at this together. Just because some bad people have a lot of money, does that mean you can't have any? No, of course not. And just because a person has a lot of money, does that automatically make them bad? Of course not. Money is money. It takes on the quality of its owner, good or bad. Just because some bad people do bad things with their money doesn't mean it's bad to have money. Am I defending the rich? No, not at all. But do I think it's fair that someone who is rich is automatically considered bad? No, I don't.

I wrote this book because I've seen the power of money, good and bad. The path I'm advocating is for you to make money. Candidly, I want you to make a lot of it, and then use it for good. That's how change occurs. Money is no doubt the most powerful lever for positive change that exists.

Along with you, I'm limited to twenty-four hours in a day, seven days per week. While there are many things I see in the world I don't agree with, I've had to conclude that I have some influence, but very little control over them. That was a tough realization, but it's true. That's why I like to be a student in many aspects of my life. Simply observing and asking questions of others is the way I learn. Perhaps the most telling truth I've come to recognize is that when it comes to changing someone else or myself, odds are much higher I can effect more change in myself. Self-transformation is hard enough, much less the challenge of convincing others to change.

I want to be the change I want to see in the world. I'm borrowing this quote, usually attributed to Ghandi. For me, it means I am choosing to make money while paying my fair share of taxes (and not a penny more), rewarding my employees, and living generously. That's how I choose to fight back against bad people with money.

As you read this book, you may not be where you want to be financially. However, the fact that you're holding it in your hands tells me you want something more—not just more money, but more impact with your money. I want you to have both. Revolutions begin when people who feel there is a better way come together to create change.

For a moment, set aside what is or is not in your bank account. Start with your heart. Enough with letting your past moves with money hold you back or paint a limited future. It's time for you to chart a new path.

I know there are many people hurting financially. Many have lost their jobs or have faced some other unprecedented life change that flat out blindsided them. As you read this book, you'll begin to learn what's in my heart for my fellow human being, and I'm willing to bet you share some of those same desires. Think of it like this: While many people trapped in poverty can't afford this book, you can be an agent of change. Someone once told me, "How can someone pull themselves up by their bootstraps if they don't even have boots?" His words were piercing. You can be the person who puts these principles into practice and pays them forward to the very people who need them most. After all, good financial advice shouldn't be reserved for the select few. More than ever, it needs to be shared. That's how revolutions begin— when the pain is great, that's when change occurs.

CHAPTER 21

Mind Your Own Business

YOUR BELIEF ABOUT what it means to be rich probably isn't true.

After all, doesn't everyone who is rich have a two-story house and a new car and dress in Gucci and Louis Vuitton? Actually, no.

In Texas, there is a term that gets bounced around a lot: "Big hat, no cattle." It refers to a person who has all the outward appearances of money—the big car, the big house, the big bling-bling—but if you dig a little deeper, their financial situation isn't, well, all that big. I have encountered a lot of people like this in my professional life. More times than not, when the person dropped the mask of affluence and was honest about his or her finances, something else was revealed.

One potential client, a doctor, earned one million dollars per year. By most people's standards that would be a dream come true. But there was a problem—a really big one. He spent more than one million dollars each year. You don't have to be a math teacher to see what's wrong. On the outside, he looked like he had it all together. But on the inside, his castle was crumbling and he had to keep spending to support his self-induced luxury lifestyle.

The moment of truth came when I asked him and his wife what would be the greatest service I could provide for them.

While they were comfortable baring their financial souls, they were less than enthusiastic to alter their financial goals. I shared several practical steps that could quickly and positively benefit them. A moment passed before they shrugged and exhaled deeply. The doctor's wife chimed in first, but with a nod of his head, the doctor obviously agreed with her concern. "How would it look if we downsized our lifestyle?" she asked, and not even rhetorically. "His patients might think his business was struggling." He added, "And how would it look to our friends? They would think something was wrong, like we're suddenly broke."

You'd think I would have been more surprised hearing their defense, but I had heard this song played many times before. I replied, "So you want the look of success but not the reality of true financial freedom?" Reluctantly, they began to understand what I was saying, but I hadn't convinced them to change their ways. "What you're saying makes sense and we know you're right, but we're just not ready to make these changes," they admitted.

When they left my office that day, it pained me. Every interaction I have with clients is very personal, and this one was no different. I knew what they needed to do. *They* knew what they needed to do. But until the pain is great, the change does not occur. And their pain was simply not great enough. I told them to call me back in six months. I've yet to receive their call.

So what does their story mean to you? People's perceptions were very important to them. Many people are buying things they don't need with money they don't have to impress people whose opinions don't pay the bills. While this couple may have been making quite a bit of money, they could barely cover their expenses. This kind of behavior is a recipe for financial disaster.

On the other side of the coin, there are people whom you might perceive as "average," but who are actually quite wealthy. These people just live well below their means. They sit next to you at your son's football game or at the PTA meeting. They stand in line behind you at the coffee bar and shop at the same discount clothing store. They've most likely worked hard, saved a lot, and simply spend less than they earn. They could afford the newest luxury car, but they choose to drive an older model sedan. These choices allow them the ability to pay cash for their kids' college education or take their grandkids to Disney World. They are choosing to master their money and not be mastered by it.

A study of over ten thousand millionaires by Ramsey Solutions revealed that nearly eight out of ten did not receive any inheritance from their parents or any other family member. Instead, it took them each an average of twenty-eight years before achieving millionaire status. Most of them reached that milestone at age forty-nine after working hard, saving, and smart investing.[1] Makes this feel a lot more attainable, right? It is—and I want to help you get there.

Part of changing your money mindset is rewriting your definition of the word "rich." What if true wealth meant living a comfortable lifestyle with the ability to generously give money away and make an impact on the world?

In my professional role as an investment advisor, those I've met along the way who are lying to themselves about their financial situation are operating out of fear, not perfidy. The only way to overcome financial fear is with financial courage. Identify what has held you back, face those issues *head* on, and *move* on. Ask yourself, "What are my financial burdens right now? What financial issues do I worry about all the time? What keeps me up at night?" That's your starting place for making changes. Your first step is to identify your most pressing challenges and goals, make your plan of attack, launch the attack, and monitor the progress of that attack.

Each of us thinks differently about money. The *Good Money Revolution* is intended to be as much purposeful as it is motivational. Motivation can come and go, but if you have a purpose, you'll fight for it. When you embrace what matters to you, *that* gives you purpose. You fight, you sacrifice, you do whatever it takes to climb the hill.

Comparison really is the thief of joy. We've all been in the space where we are jealous of what someone else has. We've been envious. We've thought to ourselves, *Why not me?* But when you focus your energy on what someone else has, you spend less time working on what you want to attain for yourself. Often the grass that's so green on the other side of the fence is actually fake, especially in this age of social media where everybody is pretending to be a millionaire. Everyone is a successful investor, everyone's business is booming. There are no sad stories on Instagram or Facebook. Everybody is just doing amazing. And *none* of it is true.

Steve Jobs, founder of Apple, once said, "Your time is limited, so don't waste it living someone else's life." Being fixated on other people's supposed success will steal your joy and your focus, allowing what you need to be doing for your own success to fall by the wayside. Celebrate other people's wins and successes. Don't let them be a distraction from what it is that you want to accomplish for yourself. Mind your own business and stay focused. There are many ways to be successful.

Stay true to you—it's often where the money appears.

CHAPTER 22

Five Attitudes about Money that Hold You Back

MY VOICEMAIL LIGHT was blinking. Catching up at the office on a Saturday morning, I pressed "play" and heard a woman's frantic voice. It was Nancie, one of my clients. She said she had bounced a check and was worried it would ruin her credit—and might even get her hauled off to jail. By the end of her message, Nancie seemed to be convinced that she would spend the rest of her life in prison.

I quickly called her back. She was startled to hear my voice. Nancie said she hadn't known whom to call, so she called me, her investment advisor. She told me she had moved money from her savings to her checking account to cover some big purchases. She assumed all was fine until she received a non-sufficient funds notice in the mail, and it had really freaked her out.

I calmed her, assuring her that she had more than enough money to cover the check and that we would call the bank together on Monday morning to move the money to the proper place. Once I assured Nancie that she would not be swapping her home for a jail cell, she was relieved. But I was curious. Bouncing a check is irritating, but how did it get elevated in her mind to such a life-changing event? So I asked her. She said she had grown up poor. As a child, she witnessed her father receiving a call for accidentally bouncing a check written to a local store to purchase school supplies for her. The store manager had threatened to call the police. While her dad was shaken, he quickly corrected the oversight. The problem was solved, but what she saw was cemented in her mind: bounce a check, go to jail. This was a successful fifty-seven-year-old woman and in an instant, she flashed back forty-eight years. By the end of the call, she was calm and thankful, yet it showed us both how her past money beliefs still caused her to react today.

Another story—this one about two friends (we'll call them John and Greg) who no longer speak to each other. John grew up in rural Iowa in a family of farmers. John and Greg were childhood friends and did everything together. Later in life, Greg had an entrepreneurial idea that grew into a successful business. John could not understand how his friend could have become so financially successful. Greg wasn't even fabulously wealthy, but John couldn't get it out of his head that Greg had more money than he did. Inexplicably, John began to believe Greg must have done something illegal to make so much money, and his accusations severed their relationship. Because of the deeply rooted money beliefs John grew up with, he couldn't accept that Greg could have become so much more financially successful than he was. John's money mindset held him back—and ruined a thirty-year friendship.

In both stories, Nancie and John's money mindsets had unintended consequences. I never want you to feel the panic and anxiety Nancie felt that Saturday morning or the jealousy and resentment John felt toward Greg. Negative feelings toward money and those who have it will sabotage your personal success and hold you back.

Stories like these are all too common—and it's just not right. Now let's dive a little deeper and investigate five different beliefs about money that could be holding you back.

1. Money represents scarcity and strain.

Because you grew up in a family that didn't have as much money as some, your parents villainized money rather than teaching you how to make it. You heard frequent arguments about not having enough. The blame, frustration, and accusations over who was spending too much caused anger and conflict. If you knew a family member or friend who lost a job or was facing a significant financial hardship, you might have seen the damage it did to their family and you began to associate pain with a lack of money. You were raised to believe that since your family didn't have money, it would always be a struggle and there would never be enough. Money represented scarcity and strain.

2. You see money as working against you.

You believe the daily grind of a job you don't like is the only way to make ends meet. You work hard for every dollar you earn. At the end of the day, money is simply a revolving door that never stops. The bills keep coming and there is always something more to pay for. It comes in and goes right back out and you have nothing to show for it. You have to keep working harder and longer to try to earn more.

It feels like you never stop working but your money isn't working for you. You think, *I don't understand how I can make more money. I have a nine-to-five job. I work, I come home, I pay the bills. I'm never truly getting ahead; I'm just treading water.* The cycle seems like it will never end.

3. Your family's money tree did not grow.

Growing up, you heard it said at the dinner table that in life, there are the "haves" and the "have-nots." You are who you are and no matter how hard you work, you won't get to enjoy the life that wealthy people have. Your entire life you've seen your grandparents and parents struggle financially. From one generation to the next, the same message gets passed down: that's just the way it is and don't expect it to change. The rich get richer, and the rest of us keep working harder.

You believe money is for other people. You see other people have it, you don't, and that's the way it is. Even if you had money, you worry what others would think of you and that you might become someone they don't like. You will be criticized for how you spend your money and feel pressured to live like others expect. It would be better not to try at all than to fail and be despised by your peers.

4. There's not enough money to fulfill your dreams.

You're stuck in your job so you can pay your bills. Sure, you've dreamed of owning your own business or doing something you really love. But where would the money come from? Who can really quit their job to pursue a dream and still pay the bills? People who must have a wealthy parent. You don't have that luxury. Plus, you don't know how to manage money and fear you will look foolish making bad decisions, or even worse, losing it all. You feel overwhelmed by financial-speak and are frustrated that you can't find a simple plan you understand. You are concerned you will spend it all and have nothing to show for it. Dreams die. Work goes on.

5. The money math doesn't add up.

Deep inside, there are causes you feel passionate about that you would love to support, but you believe only wealthy people can make a real difference. You know your money math, and giving some away doesn't add up. Plus, you don't feel in control of your money and worry if you will have enough to do the things you want to do. You are concerned about being taken advantage of and that the recipient of your giving will not work as hard with your money as you worked to earn it. Besides, if you did give your money away, people would only start asking for more. Let's be real. Can your money really change the world?

Spoiler alert: Yes, it absolutely can.

For years I watched many clients progress from the belief that money was bad to making it, investing it, and giving away more than they ever dreamed possible. But first they had to recognize and overcome their deeply ingrained negative money beliefs.

As you read through these five beliefs, you probably replayed some painful memories from your childhood (or even adult-hood). It may have felt uncomfortable and challenging to take in—but you did it anyway. I applaud you for confronting these beliefs.

I have good news for you: change starts now. But changing your money mindset isn't a one-time fight. It's a continuous battle to combat beliefs that have been deeply ingrained in you from a young age.

Your job is to flip your money script.[1] I'm about to show you how.

CHAPTER 23

Flip Your Money Script

MY HAT GOES off to the men and women who wake up every morning and commute to a job they can barely tolerate. They return home at 6:00 p.m. with the emotional baggage of leaving a place they didn't want to go to in the first place. They see their life as a revolving door. Money comes in and goes right back out—and usually there is more month left than there is money.

The result is anguish and anger toward money. Family relationships sometimes sour because everyone is constantly worried about where the next dollar will come from. With that mentality, you're just thinking about how to make ends meet, not how you can change the world. When a person, especially a child, hears this, they begin to think there's a ceiling to their success. Stories like this really pain me.

Thinking back to my own childhood, I grew up in a classic middle-class family. My dad would leave early in the morning and return home about 5:30 p.m. My mom worked part-time in retail and often had a snack waiting for my sister and me when we walked in the door from school. We lived in a modest house, and I was proud of it.

Growing up, however, I remember making judgments about people. If I saw a fellow student come to school with a new pair of the hottest shoes, I thought to myself, *Wow, they must have money; my family could never afford that.* I remember the first time I went to a friend's house that had more than two bathrooms. I thought to myself, *Wow, these people must be rich!*

These kinds of observations lead to perceptions we form as kids. Reflecting back, these memories are as real to me today as they were then. When I was just out of college, I remember driving with Kara through the neighborhood where we live today, thinking, *Wow, how could someone possibly afford these houses, and what job do they have to be able to live here?*

I wasn't satisfied to drive away and always wonder. I wanted to live in that neighborhood one day. I wasn't sure how, but I believed I could figure it out.

Ramit Sethi, who has taught thousands to manage their personal finances, believes the toxicity of money begins with one's self-identity. "When I was in college," he explains, "I used to joke that I was just a skinny Indian guy. And I wish that I could go back in time and shake my old self and tell him to stop saying that. Because . . . it became a self-fulfilling prophecy. . . . I had created my own mental cage. And many of us do the same with money. We will literally point-blank say, 'Well, I'm just not good with money.' Well, guess what? Every time you say that, it's becoming more true."[1]

Ramit also stresses that toxic ideas about money are holding people back. "We grow up believing that . . . money causes stress," he explains. "'More money, more problems.' We believe that 'I don't deserve to make more money.' And we also normalize some of our own financial situations. 'Yeah, I might have ten thousand dollars of credit card debt, but at least I don't have twenty, like Michelle. I'm fine. I'm doing okay.'"[2]

A healthy relationship with money often begins with a proper perspective of oneself. My friend Donald Miller wrote a book called *Scary Close*. In it, he says so many of us walk around thinking we are a nuisance to other people, that we're inconveniencing them. But what if that thinking were flipped and instead we thought, *You know what? I am valuable. People like me*. Don writes, "It's a beautiful moment when somebody wakes up to this reality, when they realize God created them so other people could enjoy them, not just endure them."[3]

Once you are comfortable with yourself and recognize that people value you, that leads to making more confident personal and financial decisions. You *do* help make people's lives better. Adopting this positive mindset translates into confidence and self-esteem. With that kind of attitude, your earnings are bound to skyrocket.

But maybe you've made one or more money decisions that cost you. It caused you to feel embarrassed and angry, and now you have a "once bitten, twice shy" response. This is where your redemption story gets written. Accept that it happened. What did you learn from it, as painful as it was? What would you do differently? The cold, hard truth is this: You have to get back up, brace yourself, and move forward—with your life and your money. If not, you will remain stuck. The most successful, well-admired people in the world will often tell you they've made many more mistakes than they've had successes. But they keep learning from their missteps while continuing to put one foot in front of the other. That's what I'm asking you to do right now.

I love owning a home. I hate home repairs. I learned a long time ago that the small things that need repair should really be repaired. If ignored, what would have been little fixes often turn into big problems. Our lives can look like that—hiding all the little holdbacks that add up to one big one. Maybe it was a teacher in school who said, "You are not smart." Maybe it was a parent at the dinner table who said, "Our family is just not good with money." Or your supervisor at your job stated, "Listen, you'll never get promoted. You don't have what it takes." These recordings play over and over in our heads, and we don't even realize how costly they are to our success until we get angry when we see other people living the life we want.

Popular speaker and author (and table tennis expert) Jon Acuff, wrote a book called *Soundtracks*. During an interview he told me, "Negative thoughts find you; positive thoughts we have to look for."[4]

Retraining your brain to have a positive mindset about life and money takes work. Are you willing to do it? I believe in you. If I can do it, you can too. Like millions of other Americans, through hard work and determination, I created wealth for my family and a lifestyle that is significantly improved over what I had as a child. I know you want the same for your children.

The circumstances you were born into were out of your control. Your circumstances have influenced your view of money and may have limited your potential and success. I hope you realize that regardless of where you are right now as you read this, your background, past failures, or whether you're twenty, forty, sixty, or eighty years old, you have the ability to recraft any beliefs about money that you've lived with up until today.

Now is the time. Flip your money script. Don't let it end with you.

CHAPTER 24

I Was Blind, Now I See: The Money Talk

A FEW YEARS ago when my son Conner was learning to drive, we'd go practice together, him at the wheel and me with my imaginary brake. One day as we reached a stop sign, he gently slowed but didn't come to a complete stop. Just a couple seconds later we saw a police car in our rear-view mirror flashing its red and blue lights. We were pretty sure he wasn't stopping us to say hi.

After explaining that we were father and son and that Conner was practicing his driving, the officer looked bemused (or maybe sympathetic) and gave us a break. He let Conner off with a warning and told him to make sure he came to *complete* stops in the future.

Afterward, I asked Conner why he hadn't come to a complete stop.

"Well, Dad, that's what you do at a stop sign."

That hit me right between the eyeballs. He saw my blind spot. He was right, of course. Since then, I've made it a point to treat a stop sign just like it says: I *stop* (not California style). I've also tried to translate this lesson into other parts of my life, namely by not *teaching* one thing and *doing* another.

Just like my son imitated my incomplete stops, your children are watching you—including how you deal with your money and your attitudes about it.

As a parent, you teach your kids all the things you're supposed to:

- Don't hit your sister.
- Say "please" and "thank you."
- Chew with your mouth closed.
- Drive carefully (and stop at all the stop signs).
- Nothing good happens after midnight.

But the one thing most families leave to chance is any kind of lesson about money. Often, the excuse is, "Well, we don't talk about politics or religion," and money just gets lumped in with that forbidden fruit. We fight about it with our spouses. We're reluctant to talk about it with our friends—and definitely with our kids—and that's a terrible mistake.

So what's holding you back? Number one: fear of looking incompetent when it comes to money. "I don't have all the answers," you tell yourself. "I don't know all that technical information about stocks, bonds, and interest rates. I don't speak finance. Terms like accelerated depreciation, APR, and stop limit orders mean very little to me. If I don't know all there is to know about money, how can I teach someone else?" Or you might say to yourself, "I didn't make very good money decisions, so what could I possibly teach my kids?"

This belief will keep you and your family from building real wealth. If you don't believe you can earn, save, and give more—you won't. Instead, I challenge you to hit your reset button and say out loud, "I might not know everything, but I want to learn.

I want the tools to earn more, save more, and give more so my money can impact my family and the world."

Here's the best part: You and your family can talk through this journey together—learning as you go. In the world we live in, it's difficult to admit you don't know everything. To learn a new skill or start a new job requires curiosity, humility, and discomfort. "Let's be curious together," financial coach Kelsa Dickey likes to say. Be upfront with your family. Let them know you've made mistakes and are continuing to learn.[1]

It is not uncommon to find that people (even in the same household!) have vastly different views on saving and spending, investing and giving. How can those with opposing opinions on how to handle money learn from one another? Open dialogues are the key. Seek to understand different viewpoints about money and strive to find a common ground.

Children see how their parents, grandparents, and other relatives operate with money. If they hear constant complaining and sense a scarcity mentality, they are learning, "Oh my goodness, that's how money is. It's something that brings hardship to people and makes people angry." It's important to teach them that doesn't have to be your future or theirs. Money is a tool; not a tool to be used against people, but to improve people and the world. Discussing money—why it's important, the good it can do, how to make it and save it, and how to share it with others— can truly change the trajectory of your life and the lives of your children.

You may not feel confident to speak about money, much less teach others about it. Think about all the new things you are learning. People learn a language. They learn a trade or a new skill, and the more they use that new knowledge, the more they practice it, the more skilled they become. It's the same with money. The more you learn, the more you use that knowledge, the more skilled you become, and the better money decisions you will make. Now more than ever, you, and those you care about, deserve to be equipped with the tools available to do the best you can with your money.

Keeping with the theme of driving, my youngest son, Dillon, recently earned his driver's license. As he prepared to take his driver's test in my wife's SUV, his most challenging task was to parallel park. To get ready, he would drive me to the local elementary school where I would place cones that represented cars. It was his job to skillfully back into the space while avoiding knocking over the cones, then stopping smoothly next to the curb. At first, he kept hitting the curb or running over the cones. He needed to learn to turn the wheel a little sharper. After lots of practice (and several trips to the elementary school), he began to get it. He figured out the exact spot where to pull up and stop and when to turn his wheel so that the SUV would end up nestled tightly near the curb. Suddenly he saw it, the pattern of successful parallel parking. By doing the same thing over and over—and doing it better and better—he was getting the desired result. You could say it clicked, the lightbulb went off, he got it—any catchphrase will do. When he saw success, it built confidence. So I wasn't surprised when the no-nonsense state trooper gave him a near-perfect score. The more you practice, the more skilled you become.

In that same way, you need to take the time to learn about money and the power for good that can be harnessed by using it well. Imagine if we began talking about money in ways that are constructive:

- Here's how you can make it.
- Here's how you can grow it.
- Here's how we can collaborate to do more with it.

When it comes to money, you can create your own pattern or copy someone else's. You'll likely knock over a few cones and scuff your tires on the curb. But with each attempt, you make adjustments and get closer to your goal.

Teach your kids and grandkids that money is not the enemy—that it's not money's fault you can't do something. Money is a tool. You can make it, grow it, give it—and make the world a better place.

Next, I want to give you three easy money lessons that no one is teaching your children.

CHAPTER 25

Three Money Lessons Nobody Is Teaching Your Kids

A S A PARENT, you want your kids to reach their full potential and make a difference in the world. You know that being successful with money is an important part of achieving that goal. You want them to get a good job, to be able to buy a home, provide for their family, and have a bright future. They deserve every opportunity for success, and you want them to be financially independent. Money is good, and the more your children have, the more good they can do—not only by providing a better-quality life for their own family someday, but by making a lasting impact on the world.

But someone has to teach them how to do that—and that someone can be you. Even if you don't feel equipped to teach them how to make it, save it, or invest it, I'm about to reveal three life-changing lessons to teach your kids about money. If you teach these lessons to your kids (and to yourself), they can enjoy the life you want for them and the life they want for themselves.

1. Be an investor, not a spender.

You've told your kids, "Spend less than you earn," "Avoid credit card debt," "Save for an emergency," "Use your money wisely."

That's all good advice. But how your kids put those ideas into motion has a huge impact on how much wealth they will build.

With each purchase, make a point to answer these questions: "Does this purchase add value?" "Is this an impulse buy, or will I be glad I bought this two weeks from now?" "Do I have enough cash to pay for this—even if I use a credit card to earn the points?"

There are some great places to get a cup of coffee nowadays. If you spend $5 a day on a cup of coffee, that's $35 per week, $140 per month, and more than $1,800 per year. Expenses add up—and swiping a credit card isn't always the answer. You still need the cash to pay the bill at the end of the month. When your kids get older, go to college, or live in their first apartment, will they buy new or used furniture? When it's time to purchase an automobile, will they opt for the new car or a quality pre-owned? The principle is this: Every dollar they spend is an investment in something. Asking these questions lays the groundwork to becoming a savvy spender and a wise investor.

"Like a duck on a June bug," is what Mrs. Hunt, my high school economics teacher, would say when she wanted us to get focused in her class. Years later, as each of my four children turned sixteen, we got focused fast. Our strategy was to find a quality pre-owned vehicle with low mileage that would carry them through college. I had a 50 percent success rate due to two mistakes. First, I bought a new car with great reviews, but it quickly became unreliable. Second, I purchased an older vehicle that began to rack up repairs soon after we bought it. I learned that pre-owned, low-mileage vehicles from a dependable manufacturer are a better value and last longer. I don't always make perfect money decisions either.

The lesson wasn't only that a new car loses significant value the moment you drive it off the lot. The more valuable lesson for myself and my children was to witness the decision-making process—to see what worked and what didn't and how to negotiate. These skills will serve your children well as they advance in life and could save—or cost—your children thousands.

Evaluating purchases is important, as is the attitude you convey. Telling your children, "Yes, because we budgeted for it," rather than "No, because it's not in the budget," sends a powerful message.

The principle you're teaching them is this: every dollar they spend is an investment in something that could be working for them. Are they making purchases that gain or lose value? The goal is not necessarily to do one or the other; rather, the goal is learning to make smart decisions after weighing the information.

2. Be a confident wealth builder.

You make money twice. First, you work hard to earn it. Then, you work hard to invest it wisely. Build assets. Reduce liabilities. These four words can make you and your children a lot of money. Sounds simple, but few people know how to do it. By placing your hard-earned money into a custom-tailored strategy that includes selected real estate, growth investments, and maybe even building a business of your own, you can build lasting wealth. Making consistent, deliberate decisions is the key to more money.

- **Step one:** Pay yourself first by setting and forgetting. Set up automatic payroll deductions into your company's retirement account or an automatic bank draft to move money from your checking account into an investment account on a specific day each month. If you have younger children, open a savings account for them and decide together on an amount they will save from gifts, allowance, and/or small jobs. Commit to that money going to savings first, before any is allowed to be spent.

- **Step two:** Be a generous giver. Encourage your children to give away 10 percent of the money they receive. They can give to a church, a community organization, or a cause important to them. They could even purchase supplies for a homeless shelter, an animal rescue, or a school-supply drive for disadvantaged kids.
- **Step three:** Budget, baby! Create a livable budget that encourages your kids to spend less than they earn. Reinforce agreed upon dollar amounts for saving and giving. Encourage them to pay for manageable expenses such as eating out, gas, and entertainment.

3. Be the creator of money, not the receiver of it.

You work hard to provide for your family and to make a better life for your kids than you had growing up. Unless you work for yourself, you receive a steady paycheck from your employer. But you are making money for someone else. You are the *receiver* of money.

Today's generation needs to learn that by taking the first steps toward building their own business, they can become the *creator* of money. You may have never owned a business, so how can you guide your kids? By learning about it together. Suggest that they keep their day job while starting their own side gig. Here's a modern reality: Job security is no longer a guarantee. Your children are one global event away from losing their employment.

Depending on someone else for your paycheck is placing too much control in someone else's hands. Teach your kids to begin thinking like a business owner in their current job and begin to take steps to explore their own venture.

Firefighters have modeled this approach for years. Many have launched successful moving and lawn care businesses that they run on their days off. Teachers often develop teaching materials to sell online or start after-school and summer tutoring businesses.

Many parents feel ill-equipped to teach their children about owning a business. You may have never owned a business yourself and have no idea how to even get started.

But you have skills, expertise, experience, and YouTube. There are resources available. You can do this!

My oldest daughter, Lauren, worked at a snow cone stand in high school. She observed that some employees wasted time by staring at their phones, while she always followed the philosophy, "If there's time to lean, there's time to clean." The owner noticed. The following summer, she asked Lauren to be in charge of hiring people, which stretched her. The next summer she was asked to be the social media manager and finally, the daytime manager. Every day after work, we talked about her shift and the things she could do to improve sales and customer retention. Lauren chose to work as if she were an owner. It paid off—with more responsibilities and more money.

Money is a game. Learning and implementing these three money ideas will help your kids win by giving them access to opportunities that will help secure their future and do more good in the world.

CHAPTER 26

The Power of the Screwup

ONE DAY IT hit me. I decided to give my kids "the gift of Dad." I knew they would be so excited. By the "gift of Dad," I meant that I wanted to teach and share with them all the things about money my own dad hadn't shared with me. What an incredible advantage they would have. I just knew they couldn't wait to get started unwrapping this priceless gift.

Some dreams die more quickly than others.

Kara and I had just purchased a new home. We were living in a rental house temporarily due to a nine-month gap between selling our old house and the new house being ready for us to move into. The rental house was quite small, our kids were still pretty young, and the changes completely disrupted our family routine. The close proximity to one other had its advantages though. We were always bumping into one another.

One evening I asked my daughter Lauren, in the sixth grade at the time, "Can I talk with you about something?"

"Sure," she said, as I stood at the doorway of her room.

"I want to talk to you about money," I told her. I already felt triumphant, like I was the newly crowned champion who was about to share his secrets of success. I began to share my insights on sound investing and ways to make money grow.

Well, you know that sound when something screeches to a halt, like stopping short when someone suddenly runs out on the street right in front of you, or the sound of chalk against a chalkboard? That's pretty much what happened in my mind as Lauren gave me the equivalent of a stiff arm. It wasn't exactly a physical hand to my face, but after two words of my sage advice, the blank expression on her face telegraphed, "Dad, I'm not interested. I'm bored, my eyes are closing. Take your words elsewhere."

I was surprised, then a little offended. I politely excused myself from the room. I don't give up easily, so I rethought my game plan. A few days later I tried a different approach. "Lauren," I said again. "Got a second? I want to ask you about something."

She seemed wary, but said "Okay," as I again stood in the doorway of her room.

Take two!

I mentioned to her that I thought she might find the high school Business Club I had started at her school interesting. She was only three years away from starting high school. I felt this was a great time to spark her interest and get her commitment to join. (Okay, so maybe I *was* jumping the gun a little.) "We're doing some very cool things," I told her.

"Like what?" she asked, without much expression.

"We talk about how to make money and how to start a business," I said. I gave her some examples of business success stories. I even mentioned that everyone got their favorite candy when they came to Business Club. I was sure the hook was set, but I figured that was enough for now. I didn't want to overplay my hand.

A few weeks later, I brought up the Business Club again and it piqued her interest a bit more.

"How do you get into the club?" she asked. (Probably to find out how to get the candy.)

"Well, it's not for everybody," I told her. I was brilliantly playing hard to get. I explained it was forty minutes every other week, and there was homework. She didn't seem to like the homework idea (I'm not sure why), but I assured her the homework was fun, like how to turn $5 into $25 in a single weekend.

I was sure I had her—hook, line, and sinker.

Three years later, Lauren was sitting in the first row of the first Business Club meeting of her freshman year.

Throughout high school, Lauren became a sponge, learning lots of business principles. The door had been opened for many wonderful conversations I never anticipated. Fast forward to today. I believe the Business Club and the ongoing dialogue that ensued helped shape her into the young woman she has become. More recently, helping her open her first investment account and make her first stock purchases put another smile on this dad's face.

Building curiosity is one thing; *sharing* curiosity is another, and it's a rich opportunity for learning. It's not always what you know; it's often what you don't know and can learn together. Let's say a family member has asked for your help in investing or starting a business, but you have limited to no knowledge where to begin. You could say, "Sorry, I can't help you" or you could say, "That sounds interesting. Let's learn together." The beauty of that second response is that it takes you off the hook for not being an expert. It's enough just to be an expert at empathy and to be excited about learning together.

Many—actually, most—of my clients told me they never heard their parents talk about money. It's important that you *do*. Let your children observe you and your spouse having a budget meeting. Kelsa Dickey says to let them overhear you sit down together and say things like, "Mommy needs to update her budget."[1] Children need to know that managing money takes effort, and that you don't have to have all the answers to teach somebody something.

It's also important to teach your children the personal responsibility that comes with *having* money. Bola Sokunbi says she's teaching her kids that money is power. "Having money gives them the opportunity to have options. But it's not just about *having* money, but it's about understanding how *impactful* money can be in their lives and understanding responsibility when it comes to wealth. And these options are so important because they can put their money towards causes and things that they support . . . [and] they walk away from situations or jobs that don't serve them because they know they have money in the bank."[2]

Kelsa Dickey, with a different life experience, has another equally instructive message that she wants to convey to her children. As they got older, Kelsa feared that if her business became too successful, her daughter would grow up selfish, spoiled, and entitled, without a strong work ethic. Any success Kelsa had in business had been her own doing, so she wasn't so much anxious about how *she* would handle wealth as much as how her children would handle it. She spoke to her husband about her concerns, and the two of them discussed how a child's value system and what they care about in life comes from the parents—not from money. It comes from parents teaching a work ethic, as well as empathy and compassion, regardless of whether the family is poor, middle class, or wealthy.

That was exactly what Kelsa needed to remember. "Money is neutral," she said. "Money doesn't say you have to be entitled or selfish or spoiled. . . . That was the money block that I personally had to overcome."[3]

Kelsa and her husband then did something I recommend to others. They wrote what she described to me as a family creed or motto. "Here are the values that we are going to live our life by.

And these are the values we're going to put our money behind, these are the values we're going to parent our children by, and we are going to embody these in all ways—money is just one of those ways that we will embody these. So the way we take care of ourselves, the way we take care of our home, the way we treat others—we will embody these values in all ways. And that has [been] really powerful for lots of conversations."[4]

Kara and I regularly remind ourselves to have open conversations with our kids about money too. When I decided to sell my business, we gathered the family together and told them our decision. They asked a lot of questions, like "What's next for Dad?" We were honest that we did not know the answers to a lot of their questions. Or several years ago, when Kara and I decided to give away our long-saved kitchen renovation money to help fund a gymnasium at our church, we discussed the decision as a family.

But not all moments make the highlight reel. There have been times when I made a bad decision about a particular stock and chose to share my disappointment with them. This is actually an incredibly powerful tool as well.

When you choose not to hide your money mistakes in the closet, it relieves the pressure for you to be perfect. Instead, it creates an open, safe dialogue. Let me give you an example. When I come home from the office—which these days is upstairs—it's normally dinner time. We go around the table asking, "How was your day?" If I say, "Oh, I had a good day," my kids might give me a little of their attention. But if I say, "You know what, guys? I really screwed up today," suddenly they're all ears. They're on the edge of their seats thinking, *What's Dad going to say? Dad says he screwed up? How good is this going to be?*

I call this the power of the "screw up." Most people miss out on it. When—not *if*—you screw up, you should share (if appropriate) the mistake with your family. So much of our lives are spent placing an aura around ourselves of the persona we want to be. I think that's kind of sad.

A good friend of mine told me many years ago, "Derrick, people like imperfect people better." When he said that, relief washed over me. Think about this: When you go to a friend's house and there are a couple dishes in the sink, or maybe a pillow not puffed perfectly, do you feel more at home than when you go and you feel like the home has been staged by a real estate agent? It's not uncommon that you might see a few dirty socks scattered around the Kinney home. (Hey, I still have teenage boys.) But as silly as it might sound, those dirty socks remind me that I don't have to fake it with my kids. It's okay not to have it all together and to let them in on my mistakes and parenting fails. I consider it a strength, not a weakness. This is real life, and these are life lessons. I don't want to be selfish by not sharing.

When you talk about your screwups in front of your kids, they start to pay attention and respect you for your candor. Use the power of the screwup and start talking about money together.

CHAPTER 27

Turning Five Dollars into Much, Much More

ARMED WITH A stack of $5 bills in my hand one Friday afternoon, I arrived ready to dish out the cash for the Business Club $5 Challenge.

My passion runs deep for investing in the lives of young people to help them reach their full potential. One way I do that is by leading the Business Club at my children's school.

As soon as I began handing each of the forty students a $5 bill, I had their attention. "There are moments in life," I told them, "when your back is against the wall and you simply have to make something happen. What would you do if something you hold most dear were taken away from you if you didn't find a way to turn $5 into $25? I know what you'd do—you'd find a way."

I challenged them to turn the $5 into $25 over the weekend. I asked for a show of hands to gauge who would commit to making a five times return on the $5. About fifteen hands went up.

"Here's the deal," I told them. "Those of you in the room who do not want to accept the challenge, keep the $5 and do something meaningful with it. Give it away or do something nice for someone with it. For those of you who do take the challenge, you're going to learn something about yourself that will stay with you forever. You're going to feel what it's like to put pressure on yourself and make something happen. A manufactured sense of urgency can create a powerful lesson. Text me on Sunday night and tell me how you did. Oh, and by the way, you get to keep everything you make, including the $5."

I was excited to see what the students would do. Twenty-four hours later, text messages began to roll in. Some didn't quite make it to $25, but they gave good efforts. Others used the $5 to purchase something for someone else, such as an ice cream cone for their younger sister or a coffee for the person in line behind them. But there were a couple of clear winners. A young man named Clay told me that due to the recent storm that had hit our area, tree limbs and debris were still strewn across many of the yards in his neighborhood. He spent $4 on trash bags and went door to door, asking his neighbors if he could clean up their yard. In one day, he turned his $5 into $78.

A few years later, Clay asked me to write a letter of recommendation for business school. The typical reference letter validates why the applicant is a good person and a good student, but I took a different path. I told the dean how Clay had used his own creativity and ingenuity to turn $5 into $78. "If he did that with $5," I wrote, "think of what he could do with a degree from your fine business school." Clay called when his acceptance letter arrived in the mail.

Another student, Will, texted me that on Saturday he had bought a case of twenty-four bottled waters for $4.99. He sold each to sweaty parents during his sister's soccer game and grossed $40 his first day, with a net gain of $35. On Sunday, he bought a case of thirty-two waters and did the same thing, for a net gain of $42. He earned a total net profit of $77.

Sometimes we overcomplicate things. Will saw thirsty people on a hot soccer field and provided a solution that quenched their thirst. He simply saw a need and met it. By turning $5 into $77, Will won a $25 Amazon gift card and he got to keep all his profits, including the $5. But the real win was the bet he made on himself. That's an investment that will pay lifelong dividends.

My daughter Lauren also decided to take the challenge. After wrestling with what to do, she bought some cupcake mix, made three dozen cupcakes, and she and her younger sister walked the neighborhood attempting to sell them. She figured if she sold all of them for $2 each, she'd net almost $75.

At the first house she visited, a neighbor bought two cupcakes but gave her $8. She figured she was off to a good start. At the next house, Mr. Lewis asked what she was doing and why. She explained she had accepted a challenge from her school Business Club to turn $5 into $25. He asked her to wait just a moment, and when he returned, he handed Lauren a crisp $100 bill. "Now I've paid for all the cupcakes. Please go around the neighborhood and give them out for free." Lauren was stunned and ran back to our house to share the good news. She then delivered cupcakes to every neighbor on our street.

This story has several lessons baked into it. First, courage is often rewarded. Going door-to-door isn't easy, but Lauren did it. Second, it taught her a lesson that if you explain your goals, and they're worthy, people want to help. Lauren was looking to sell one cupcake, but Mr. Lewis saw a bigger and more impactful plan. Perhaps the best lesson was Lauren seeing someone spontaneously and genuinely showing unexpected generosity. He created a story that years later our family still talks about.

So you see, making money can actually be fun. But giving it away? That's even better. In Part 3, I'm going to show you why.

PART 3

Good Money Giveaway

CHAPTER 28

Giving Will Change You

I N THE MIDDLE of a humid Georgia July, Fred Barley was sleeping in a tent on the campus of Gordon State College when he was visited by police officers responding to a trespassing call. They asked Barley to leave his makeshift home but changed their approach once they heard his story. Barley had biked more than six hours to register for his second semester at Gordon State, with nothing more than two duffel bags and a box of cereal to last him for the few weeks until school started. The dorms didn't open until August, but Barley felt campus was the safest place to stay and was hoping to find a job to support himself. The police officers took Barley to a local motel and paid for two nights. Word of Barley and his determination traveled quickly throughout the community, and the owner of the motel allowed Barley to stay there until he was allowed to move into the dorms. He was also offered a job as a dishwater at a local pizzeria. What's more, the community started a GoFundMe page for Barley and raised enough to cover the cost of his tuition, living expenses, and then some. Barley's situation dramatically changed thanks to one act of generosity by two police officers.[1]

Sixteen-year-old Shane Jones was searching for a unique way to make some extra cash. After watching a few YouTube videos, he found a side hustle he didn't know existed: purchasing the contents of repossessed storage units. When a renter stops paying for the storage units, their belongings are put up for auction, and the buyer of those items can turn around and sell them for a profit. Shane bid one hundred dollars and won, but when he arrived at the storage unit, he knew he couldn't sell anything. Inside the unit were stuffed animals, photographs, and personal documents. Shane discovered the owner was in prison and realized this was probably everything that person owned. With the help of his parents, Shane tracked down the owner's mother at a retirement home and gave her the belongings. She was thrilled that someone would give their time and money just to help her incarcerated son.[2]

Colton was struggling to pay his college tuition. He had been going a semester at a time while working full-time, but money was getting tight and he wasn't sure how he was going to pay for his next semester. After church one Sunday, he walked up to the front and asked an elder to pray with him that God would provide a way for him to keep attending school. A few days later, Colton received a phone call from a woman who told him she wanted to pay for his tuition. He was speechless. Because of her generosity, Colton was able to graduate and earn a scholarship to graduate school.

Patrick's niece, Jocelyn, had just graduated high school. She was bright and a good kid, but her family struggled financially. Going to college would be a stretch, but Patrick wanted to do something meaningful for her. At the mall on a Saturday, he thought about buying a gift card to her favorite clothing store, but he realized that would just be spent and soon forgotten. As he walked by a bookstore, Patrick remembered an article he had read about opportunities for women in science, technology, engineering, and math. STEM, they called it. *She's always been strong in math*, he thought. As he perused the bookstore, he found a book on opportunities in the STEM field. Inside the book was a chapter on scholarships and grants that would really help her. Jocelyn's face lit up when her uncle handed her the book and read the handwritten note inside: "Jocelyn, I believe in you. I look forward to seeing you soar to great heights. Love, Uncle Patrick." That $20 didn't seem like much then, but the vote of confidence he gave his niece continues to pay great dividends.

We've all met people who just need one missing piece to complete their puzzle. I get emotional every time I read these kinds of stories because this is what the Good Money Framework is all about. Earning, saving, and *giving*. It's about becoming a giver so you can be a participant in stories like these.

Think about a time when someone (even a stranger) helped you or fulfilled a need. Did someone in front of you in the Starbucks drive-thru pay for your coffee? Have you been stuck on the side of the road with a flat tire and a kind stranger stopped to help you change it? It's funny how often we receive help the times when it is least expected. Maybe it was just a kind word at the right time—after a relative passed away, or when you weren't sure how much more screaming you could take from your kids, or after you'd had a terrible day at work. Whatever that moment was, a kindness most likely made you feel loved or valued—and the way you went about your day was different. Maybe you had a little more patience with your kids or smiled when the car in front of you cut you off at the stoplight.

When have you been the giver? Have you ever paid for someone's drink or bought an extra sandwich in the drive-thru for the homeless person on the corner? Have you ever donated to your local food pantry or volunteered your time for a cause you feel passionate about? You've likely walked away with a big smile on your face, knowing that you made one person's life better. Even if no one else knew about it.

Giving is powerful. It changes the trajectory of your day, and it can change the trajectory of your life.

You've now learned the savvy tricks to earn and save more. We've debunked the myth that money is bad and learned how to leverage your money mistakes to teach those around you wise money habits. Now it's time to use your money today to make a difference for tomorrow and beyond.

Since my teenage years, I've been passionate about giving. At my first job at a grocery store in Arlington, Texas, I made a whopping $3.35 an hour. Raking in the big bucks (at least I thought I was). Even back then, it was important to give a portion of what I made.

Giving made me feel like my money had infinite possibilities. When I gave money to my local church, I knew it could do things and reach people I couldn't on my own. At the local food pantry, I knew the money could stretch to feed more people than I would have been able to. It gave me great joy to take the little I had and see it be used for greater things. Deep inside, I also understood that I couldn't give more money away if I didn't earn more. That purpose fueled me to make even more money through the ways I've described in Parts One and Two.

What we do with little reflects what we would do with much. It is true for me. It is true for you. Giving is the heartbeat of the Good Money Revolution. I want you to make more and save more so you can ultimately give more to the causes that light a fire within you.

CHAPTER 29

Giving Makes You Happier and Is Contagious

IT WAS CHRISTMAS Day and our family was getting ready to volunteer at our local homeless shelter, where we expected to help distribute clothes, shoes, and other donations. My four kids had been excited to go, but since they were now snuggled on the couch with their new Christmas presents, they were less than thrilled to get up and leave.

As we were leaving the house, I shoved some cash I had received for Christmas that day into my pocket and asked my kids to do the same. "Hey," I said, addressing all four of them. "I'm bringing some of my Christmas money with me. God might ask us to give it away. You might bring yours, too, just in case."

"Dad, we're tired. Can we just stay home?" they echoed in unison.

"It's important that we go," I reminded them. "Always be open and willing to give."

My kids would tell you now that they knew I was right, but they left their Christmas cash wedged between wrapping paper and cards. We all hopped in the car and our white Suburban pulled out of the driveway.

The parking lot was packed. Wrapped around the gated fence surrounding the edges of the parking lot was a line of homeless people waiting to get inside. On the concrete lay rows and rows of donated shoes. There were kids' shoes no longer than the length of an index finger, along with adult dress shoes, slippers, and sneakers all lined up ready to be worn.

An hour flew by. My daughter Lauren was frantically hunting for a pair of men's dress shoes that would fit the homeless man who had just found pants and a suit in his size. To her right, she watched as a young volunteer walked up to the shoe pile and silently deposited his own clean, new shoes next to the homeless man's pile of clothes. Just white socks covered his feet as he walked away on the chunky concrete with a small joyful smile on his face, ready to seek out someone else who needed help. As Lauren stood there watching, tears filled her eyes. She wondered, *What if I gave freely like that?*

Another man approached my son Conner and asked if we had any size 10.5 shoes. Most of the bigger sizes had been taken, so Conner shook his head, but at the same time kneeled down and began untying his own Adidas. "Here," he said, holding the shoes out to the man. "These should fit."

Immediately another woman approached the shortened rows of shoes. "I'm looking for a size 7.5 in tennis shoes," she whispered. Lauren stepped across the row and slipped off her shoes. "These are exactly what you're looking for," she said. The woman objected, but Lauren insisted. "These are yours," she told her, and slid the shoes into the woman's bag. Without anyone else knowing, Hannah and Dillon had also slipped off their shoes and given them away.

My eyes filled with tears. Two hours before, our kids hadn't even wanted to leave the comfort of our couch, and now they were walking around in socks on the coarse concrete.

A few minutes later, Lauren turned around to see a woman facing her across the rows of women's shoes. "Hi, I'm a reporter for a local newspaper," she said. "I saw what you did just now. Why did you do it?"

Lauren smiled and told her of the man who had led by example. She had simply followed.

As a dad, my heart beams with pride when I see my kids open their hearts to others. It wasn't a million dollars or a brand-new car. It was just shoes. Replaceable. Shoes will rip and tear and get muddy and fall apart one day, but the look of shock on that man's face when Conner reached down and began untying his own shoes—I'll never forget it.

That afternoon, five members of my family walked back to our Suburban without shoes on their feet and a look of pure joy on their faces. That's the power of giving—and it all started with one stranger leading by example.

When you give, you create a ripple effect that encourages others to give. Artist Kent Youngstrom points out that generosity is not just about giving back. It's about giving forward, which can reset today's culture.[1]

In other words, giving is contagious. A study by Harvard researchers James Fowler and Nicholas Christakis, published in the *Proceedings of the National Academy of Sciences*, shows that when one person behaves generously, it inspires observers to behave generously too. In fact, the researchers found that altruism could spread by three degrees—from person, to person, to person, to person. "As a result," they write, "each person in a network can influence dozens or even hundreds of people, some of whom he or she does not know and has not met."[2]

Jesse Cole invested in a low-performing, unprofitable Minor League baseball team in Savannah, Georgia. His energy and influence turned the Savannah Bananas around, and they've had sold out games ever since. How did he do it? He put people first. "For us, making a difference in the community is one fan at a time," he said.[3] "Many people think, *I've got to start with this big cause, this big effort,* but when you impact one life at a time, that translates into multiple lives, and that reaps the benefits of what you have planted."

Jesse is right. Whether it's the shoes off your feet or the cash in your pocket, giving changes things. It changes you and the people around you. It can even transform your business and make you wealthier. But remember, money only makes you happy up to a certain point. What you do with your money—your Generosity Purpose—is much more important than how much you have.

Dr. Mike Norton reminded me that what he calls "investing in others" is an integral part of every world religion. "Every world religion and philosophy has something about not focusing on yourself and helping others," he says. "Investing in others is the idea that when we use our money to benefit other people, like buying gifts or giving to charity, again that tends to make us happier than buying another thing for ourselves."[4]

Mike is not alone in his findings. A comprehensive report published in the *Journal of Personality and Psychology* analyzed more than a dozen academic and psychological studies. Taken together, they provide evidence that human beings around the world experience emotional rewards from using their financial resources to benefit others. Among its specific findings:

- Prosocial spending, defined as using one's financial resources to help others, is correlated with greater well-being, even when allowing for income differences.
- North American students who were randomly assigned to spend a small windfall on others were significantly happier

at the end of the day than those assigned to spend money on themselves.
- Children as young as two years old exhibit increased happiness when giving a valued resource away.
- Kind acts offer emotional or recuperative benefits.
- Buying a small gift for charity leads to higher levels of positive effect than buying the same gift for oneself.
- Examining over two hundred thousand respondents drawn from 136 countries, prosocial spending was linked to higher subjective well-being around the world.
- People experience emotional benefits from sharing their financial resources with others not only in countries where resources are plentiful but also in impoverished countries where scarcity might seem to limit the possibilities of reaping the gains from giving to others.[5]

In addition, the rewarding properties of generosity can be detected at a neural level. According to a separate study supported by the National Institutes of Health, when people give to charities, it activates regions of the brain associated with pleasure, social connection, and trust, creating a "warm glow" effect. Scientists believe that altruistic behavior releases endorphins in the brain, producing the positive feeling known as the "helper's high."[6]

For his tenth birthday, my son Dillon wanted to help the homeless. Instead of birthday presents, he asked people to purchase blankets and socks. He took the donations; added peanut butter, crackers, and water bottles; and made individual bags to hand out. We kept them in the back of our Suburban, available to give to a homeless person anytime we saw one when we were out in our community. Of course, every ten-year-old kid wants birthday presents. Dillon did too. Yet he understood that the happiness from a new gift would wear off in a few days (or the gift would be broken). Helping the homeless was his Generosity Purpose. Not only did it make Dillon happy to help a problem he was passionate about, but our family and his friends loved participating in the project.

Whether it starts with a pair of shoes on Christmas Day, making a homeless pack, or simply paying for a meal for a friend or stranger, your giving makes the world better and inspires others to do the same. The act of giving changes attitudes, changes hearts, changes lives—and makes you healthier.

CHAPTER 30

Giving Makes You Healthier

NOT ONLY DOES giving make you happier, it also makes you healthier.

After Mary's husband, Richard, suddenly passed, she was drifting without a destination. She looked like she had aged a decade, her blood pressure was through the roof, and she was eating poorly. Over the next few months, I walked alongside her as she began sorting through her new life. When I asked what she enjoyed, her answer surprised me. "Baseball," she replied. She loved watching every Texas Rangers game on television. Then I asked her if there was a cause she and Richard had cared deeply about while he was still living. She told me Richard had been a dedicated volunteer at the food bank at their church.

I suggested she try to combine these two passions, and we came up with a plan. Mary had been feeling increasingly isolated since Richard had passed, and a crazy idea occurred to us. As we talked, she mentioned how much she missed being around people, and we thought about how at baseball games, there are men and women who take your tickets and show you to your seats. Then you actually get to watch the game.

"How about this?" I suggested. "Why don't you try to get a job like that at Globe Life Field [where the Texas Rangers play] and give part or all your income from working at the stadium to the church's food bank?"

Mary's eyes lit up. I helped Mary apply for the job, and a few weeks later she was directing baseball fans to their seats. Three months later she was a different person, raving about how much fun she was having at the ballpark and how much satisfaction she was getting from serving people at the food bank. She had even made a few new friends who shared her love of baseball, and she said she felt happier and healthier, and that her doctor had told her that her blood pressure had dropped significantly. "I get it now because I'm living it," she told me. "I'm making a little extra money and at the same time making the world a better place. And in the process, my life has gotten a lot better." Combining her interests with a new purpose led Mary to make new friends and enjoy the sport she loved—all while improving her health and a small slice of the world.

A physical reaction actually occurs when you are generous with both your time and money. Giving has been linked to the release of oxytocin, a hormone that induces feelings of warmth, euphoria, and connection to others. In laboratory studies, Paul Zak, the director of the Center for Neuroeconomics Studies at Claremont Graduate University, and his colleagues found that a dose of oxytocin will cause people to give more generously and to feel more empathy toward others. And those people on an "oxytocin high" can potentially jumpstart a virtuous circle, where one person's generous behavior triggers another's.[1]

I've seen this happen to people numerous times—they start giving, and they feel better both spiritually and physically. But don't just take my word for it. A wide range of research has linked different forms of generosity to better health, even among the sick and elderly:

- In his book *Why Good Things Happen to Good People*, Stephen Post, professor of preventive medicine at Stony Brook University, reports that giving to others increases health benefits in people with chronic illness, including HIV and multiple sclerosis.[2]
- A study from researchers at the University of California, Berkeley and Stanford University found that elderly people who volunteered for two or more organizations were 44 percent less likely to die over a five-year period than were non-volunteers, even after controlling for their age, exercise habits, general health, and negative health habits.[3]
- A study of elderly couples by Stephanie Brown and her colleagues at the University of Michigan found that people who provided practical help to friends, relatives, or neighbors, or gave emotional support to their spouses, had a lower risk of dying over a five-year period than those who did not.[4]
- A study by Rachel Piferi of Johns Hopkins University and Kathleen Lawler of the University of Tennessee found that people who provided social support to others had lower blood pressure than participants who didn't.[5]
- According to the Mayo Clinic, people who volunteer have lower rates of depression, lower stress levels, and may live longer.[6]

Some of the most beautiful stories I've been a part of are when I've helped people creatively combine their Generosity Purpose with a job or volunteer position they love—and I want to challenge you to do the same thing.

Before Mary and I brainstormed together, she was lonely, hurting, and unsure where her future was headed after her husband passed. But after talking with her and discovering what she loved, we landed on a fantastic solution. In Mary's case, working for her favorite baseball team while donating her income to her church's food bank changed the trajectory of her health—and her life.

Giving makes you happier, healthier, and is contagious. But that's not all. It's also one of the best ways to make more money.

CHAPTER 31

Giving Is Good Business

OVER TWENTY-FIVE YEARS ago, I became a financial advisor to help people reach the goals that were important to them. Money was the tool that could provide for their families and help them enjoy the life they'd always wanted. I was determined to help them achieve their goals by managing their money wisely.

As I got to know my clients, I came to realize something else. While there were many financial advisors my clients could work with, unbeknownst to me, I was differentiating myself from the rest of them. Like any business, my customers could just as easily buy the product or service I was selling from another investment advisor. My firm was the only firm in town that was making *giving* an important part of its investment strategy—using some of our profits to support education and causes that benefited our local community. I lost count of the number of times during my career when a client or potential client said to me, "We're working with you because we saw a picture of you in the newspaper giving an award to a student at a local school," or, "We saw you on television being interviewed about investment advice, and we've heard of your contributions to the community." The more I gave back, the more people wanted to work with me. I became the *giving investment advisor.*

The perception people have of you is important in any business—and *positive perception leads to profitability*. When people perceive you as a giver, they think of you as someone who cares about their community, and they're more likely to trust you. It makes for causal relationships because now they're not just working with you; they're working with *both* you and the causes you're a part of, and that becomes what's important to them too. They are part of something bigger.

One of the most repeated pieces of advice I've given to my kids is, "You want people to know you, like you, and trust you." This is practical life advice, but it's also good business advice. Connecting your business to your Generosity Purpose allows both potential and current customers to get to know you on a deeper level.

Let me give you an example. You're out shopping and right next to each other, there are two cookware stores. At the first store, an associate walks up to you, asks how you're doing, and tells you how nice and high quality the cookware is. "Enjoy your shopping and let me know if you need anything!" he says.

At the adjacent cooking store, an associate walks up to you, asks how you're doing, and proceeds to tell you why this store is special. "Particularly in Third World countries, many people don't have access to healthy food," he says. "As a result, children and their families are malnourished and sickly. As a company, we're passionate about doing what we can to solve this problem. That's why when you purchase anything in our store, part of the proceeds goes directly to help families struggling to find healthy food."

Which cooking store will you buy from? The second one. Why? Because you need some nice cookware and can impact the world at the same time. So you buy a pot, a pan, and a couple sets of silverware and walk out of the store pleased because you've spent money that benefited a cause you believe in. Now every time you open your silverware drawer and pull out a fork or spoon, you smile. Your purchase met a need and made a difference.

"It's good business. Giving back is, in fact, a way to get more," agrees Jason Feifer, editor-in-chief of *Entrepreneur* magazine. "You obviously have to create a sustainable business in order to operate and to do good. But what I have found over and over again in the companies that I talk to is that when they figure out ways to really connect with communities, and to really support those communities, they engage and excite their own team members, they create a better, stronger culture of people who are excited to show up to work every day and to be a part of this mission, and they also attract new customers."[1]

Feifer cites numerous research studies that demonstrate the willingness of consumers to spend more and make purchasing decisions because they feel aligned with a company's mission. "If you're gonna survive as a business in times like these, then you have to go beyond just offering a product or service. You have to be really meaningful to people in their lives. And so I think that, in a way, this is going to be a filtering moment. And the companies that are really crystal clear about their mission are the ones that are going to thrive, and the other ones may not have a place in this new world." Ultimately, as Feifer himself has said, it's not about *what* you do, it's about *why* you do it.[2]

In Part 1, I used the example of Bombas socks. For every purchase, they donate a pair of socks to someone in need. Another great example of a company that gives back is TOMS. It all started with a vacation to Argentina, where founder Blake Mycoskie met a lady who shared with him how many children lacked shoes, which exposed them to numerous diseases. He decided to create a for-profit business called TOMS, but for every pair sold, he would donate a pair of shoes to a child in need.[3]

I remember when my daughter Lauren got her first pair of TOMS. The packaging even came with a TOMS flag that she proudly hung in her room. She participated in "One Day Without Shoes," where you go without shoes for one day to experience how shoes impact almost every moment of your day-to-day life. All because Lauren knew the TOMS mission and was proud to support it. Since 2006, TOMS has impacted over 100,000,000 lives.[4]

Clearly communicating your Generosity Purpose to your customers will lead them to like you. And when they know you and like you, the next step is trust. When your customers know you, like you, and trust you, they will keep doing business with you—over and over again. Companies like Bombas and TOMS have done two things well. First, they've connected their business with their Generosity Purpose. Second, they've clearly communicated their Generosity Purpose in their marketing and advertising. It's on their website and in their stores—proudly showcased for the world to see.

In her book *Do Good at Work*, Bea Boccalandro makes a compelling case that those who pursue a social purpose, who are givers throughout their careers, end up doing better financially. "It's the power of all people living out their inner giver, getting things done," she says. "We all have that potential."[5]

And yes, studies show that unselfish people tend to earn more than selfish people. That's the conclusion of research by Stockholm University, the Institute for Future Studies, and the University of South Carolina published in *The Journal of Personality and Social Psychology*. The study defines unselfishness as the desire to help others because you care about their welfare.[6]

My friend Moody is a well-known orthodontist in my community. How did he get to be so popular? Besides excelling at his craft and creating great-looking smiles, many years ago Moody connected his dental practice to his Generosity Purpose: helping children in Africa get quality dental care. He and his family, along with dental and non-dental friends from the community, periodically set up dental clinics in rural areas where children and their families can get emergency and pain-relieving dental care. His patients are always talking to him about his experiences. You want your children to receive high-quality orthodontic care. Combine that with playing a small part in helping to make the world a better place? That's a real winner. As a business owner, it's a special moment when you experience a point of intersection between doing what you love and loving how it makes the world better.

"I believe that if you're able to love what you do and show up with intent and share way more than you think is possible to share, I believe that the wins that come out of that in the long game will flood out any short-term losses," says Charles Antis, founder and CEO of Antis Roofing.[7] This mindset began with spontaneously giving a free roof to a woman in need. After thirty years of building his company, Charles's Generosity Purpose is clear—to give more and to inspire his employees and other companies to make a difference by volunteering and giving financially to causes in their communities. His message is simple: give, give, give.

What goes around comes around, which is another way of saying, "You get what you give." For years, Ken Rusk, author of *Blue Collar Cash*, has been paying for the production of fundraising commercials for the Make-A-Wish foundation. In one, a girl named Kaylee Halko, who has progeria, a rare genetic disorder that causes children to age rapidly, was featured in a television spot. "She is the neatest young lady you'll ever meet," Ken told me.[8]

Ken explained that he didn't fund the commercial to enhance his business; it doesn't even mention his company.

"I never thought it would happen this way, but I've had many customers say, 'I called you because of that commercial, because of your willingness to give back.' So, again, you don't ever want to do charity in the hopes of getting something back—you don't wanna do that—but if it does happen, it's kind of a nice little thing to occur. But I believe in the power of good . . . and it goes all the way around."[9]

You must connect your business to your Generosity Purpose. When you do, your customers will know you, like you, trust you, and become a part of a mission you're passionate about. Plus, you will make more money while creating the impact and fulfillment you've always wanted.

CHAPTER 32

Four (Bad) Reasons for Not Giving

WHEN MY WIFE and I were newly married, we were barely making ends meet. After college, I took a job with a small technology firm. The work required long hours and I quickly became bored. My boss was infamously known for telling me and my group of coworkers on Fridays at 5:00 p.m. that we would have to stay and work the weekend. The final straw came when I was passed over for a raise; I resigned. I decided to burn the ships, take a risk, and start studying hard to become a financial advisor while Kara worked as a bank teller near our tiny apartment. Our only weekly treat was the $1.25 chips and salsa at Chili's.

Our church Sunday School class was filled with fun couples, each of us making our way in life. One early evening, high winds just about blew off the roof of the house where Reggie and Linda lived. They couldn't afford the necessary repairs; they didn't even have the money to cover their insurance deductible. After hearing their need one Sunday morning, a few couples in the class got together and decided to donate what was needed. Kara and I started giving up Chili's nights so we could pitch in. Even though we didn't have much, we had something, and we knew God could use it for something bigger than ourselves. Later that week, an anonymous cashier's check was placed in Reggie and Linda's mailbox. The next Sunday at church, they told all of us that something amazing had happened: someone had anonymously paid for their roof to be repaired. Fortunately, the rest of us had been practicing our best poker faces and Reggie and Linda never did learn who was behind the anonymous gift.

Giving may not be a normal part of your life right now. You're busy with your job, your family, and your friends, and, of course, your bills that have to be paid every month. Giving is the last thing you might be thinking about. But that changes now. Good money doesn't have anything to do with the *amount* of money you have. We've already dispelled those myths, like "Once I get a better job or a promotion and I have more money, *then* I will give," or, "Once I'm older and more comfortable, *then* I can be generous." Remember, what you do with little is what you will do with a lot. You don't have to wait to win the lottery before you can make an impact. The money you have right now can be used for good—today.

Here are the four most common excuses people use for not being generous and why they shouldn't stop you from giving.

1. If I give, I'll go broke.

When our kids were young, Kara and I decided to give them each a monthly allowance. We wanted them to start learning how to manage money early in life and that giving was just as important as getting. I gave the kids four envelopes each—one for saving, one for spending, one for tithing, and one for giving. They liked the idea until they realized most of their money wasn't meant for spending. My daughter Hannah asked, "But what if I don't have money because I give it all away?" We assured her she could creatively think of ways to make more.

Kara and I encouraged each of them to think of their Generosity Purpose and use the money to help a cause they cared about. Hannah picked World Vision, a child-sponsorship organization, and we sponsored a little girl named Naomi. Hannah loved flipping through the monthly giving catalogue and seeing all the ways her money could help Naomi and her family. She settled on a big giving goal: buying Naomi a goat. She started doing more chores around the house to earn more money, and just a few months later she had saved enough to make that special purchase. She ended up earning much more than her monthly allowance, and she was no longer afraid of losing all her money because she had learned two things: her money could change a family's life, and she could creatively think of ways to make more so she could give more.

2. How can I give to others if I can't even pay my monthly bills?

Former British Prime Minister Margaret Thatcher once said, "No one would remember the Good Samaritan if he'd only had good intentions; he had money as well." You must have money to give money, and it's time now to take the steps to get out of debt as we discussed in Part 1:

- Stop borrowing money.
- Pay off high-interest credit cards first.
- Make a budget and stick to it.
- Sell something.
- Get a part-time job.

Being in debt can feel like a weight on your shoulders that only gets heavier with time. When a client referred me to their son and daughter-in-law, I sensed their frustration immediately. Because Tom and Laura had made some poor financial moves early in their marriage, they felt every dollar of their hard-earned paychecks went to pay off debt. Nevertheless, I suggested they take 1 percent of their income and give it to a cause they cared about. "Let that be your release valve," I told them. "It will be a pocket of money that you have control over. It will help give you meaning while you're paying off your debt." Three months later when we spoke again, Tom and Laura admitted they had at first thought it was a silly idea, but that even giving such a small amount had energized them and motivated them that as they paid off their debt, they would also increase their giving.

Gerry and Samantha were in a similar place. Aggressively paying off their credit card debt was their sole focus in life. In less than six months, it would be paid off. The light was brightening at the end of the tunnel. After hearing me speak on generosity, they decided to alter their plan slightly. They started giving 10 percent to support their church's mission work. At first, it didn't make sense. Why would they give now if it might prolong their debt payoff? They realized that six months of investing in the lives of others would pass by and they would miss out on a great opportunity to start impacting the world immediately. Blessings come from unexpected places, and two months later Samantha was offered a promotion. When you're determined to improve your situation while serving others, good results tend to follow.

One of our *Good Money* podcast listeners, Jacque, told me, "My husband and I are working on saving and paying off our debt. But after listening to you talk about giving, last night we decided to take 10 percent of whatever we save each month and do something good with it. Sometimes it means putting down an extra tip at a restaurant, making a donation to a school, or donating to a cause that's important to us. It was an amazing thought to think that we can bless ourselves and others twelve times this year. Thank you for turning on that lightbulb!"

Debt didn't hold any of these people back, so why should you? Start making an impact now.

3. The desire to keep it all for yourself.

When you're making money, it's hard to take chips off the table. One year, the stock market was red hot. Several clients of mine held quite a bit of their company's stock. As the market hit new highs almost daily, I encouraged them to begin taking profits to have something to show for the money they were making on paper. One by one they all told me the same thing, "Let's wait, I think it's going to go higher." Over twenty-five years as a financial advisor taught me one thing: the stock market has a mind of its own.

Sure enough, it turned sour. In some cases, their company stock value plummeted 40 percent. All that gain, now only pain. Now they were all asking the same question: "What would I have done with that money?"

I often told clients, "I would rather have you complain to me, 'Why didn't I make more money?' than 'Where did the money go?'" Greed often leads to regret.

One of my favorite Bible stories is the parable of the rich young ruler. One day he came to Jesus and asked, "What must I do to inherit eternal life?" Jesus told him to keep the commandments, such as do not murder, do not steal, and honor your father and mother. The man responded by saying, "I've done all of those!" But Jesus told the man that he still lacked one thing: giving his riches away to the poor. The young man was struck with disappointment and walked away. He loved his treasure so much and wasn't willing to give it up.[1] It's tempting to look at the young ruler and think, "Dude! Just give some of your fortune. You already have so much." I bet you've expressed the same sentiment about wealthy billionaires and celebrities you see on social media. "Those people have too much! Why don't they give more to help others?" But I want you to ask the same question to yourself: "Am I giving?" If we look deep inside ourselves, we can relate to the young ruler. When you cash that paycheck, it's hard not to hold on to it. You want to keep it all.

There will always be a temptation not to give your money and keep it for yourself. Someone at church once told me why he gives as much as he does. "Every time I drop a check in the offering plate, it's me fighting against greed," he told me. Can I be completely candid with you? I, too, hear this voice that says, "C'mon, Derrick, do you really want to give that much away? What if something happens to your family? What if something happened to you and you couldn't work? What if . . ." The voice of Resistance (with a capital *R*), as author Steven Pressfield likes to call it, is real.[2]

Giving isn't about the cost to you. Giving is not a win/lose game. You don't lose and the organization wins. Fight against that "voice of Resistance" and start giving to a cause bigger than yourself. The impact and joy you receive is well worth it.

4. There's no evidence that giving helps.

To the contrary, evidence says giving does help. Countless non-profits and people who give are daily changing people's lives—as proven in the research referenced for this book. But I want to ask you a personal question: Hasn't giving helped *you*? When have you benefited because someone gave their money or time to make something better? I bet you can think of a time.

When my dad lost his job during my junior year in college, he and my mom had to make a difficult decision. He found a job out of state, but it meant leaving me behind while I finished school. The first Sunday at church after my parents moved away was hard. An older, caring couple invited me to lunch. During that hour at the Black-Eyed Pea restaurant, they affirmed me and breathed belief into a young man. That lunch probably cost them $35. I've had thousands of lunches since then, but that lunch, that moment, is etched in my mind forever. And it shows the power of an investment in another person. Over the years, I've taken many people to lunch to pay it forward, always remembering that couple from church who helped me.

Giving helps people. People matter. Your giving can make a big impact, even if you don't think you have much to give.

The truth is, you probably have more than you think. You're breathing right now. You have friends, you have a family, you have a place to sleep and food in your fridge. You have knowledge and experience. You are skilled at something. So test it out. Buy a burger at a fast-food restaurant for the car behind you. Volunteer at your local homeless shelter and pick up a couple of toothbrushes to donate on the way. Teach a child in your neighborhood how to bake cookies and share them with those who live on your block. You have something to give. And it *does* make a difference.

Don't let these four mindsets hold you back from living a life of impact. Life is all about giving. Everyone is better because of it.

CHAPTER 33

Plan Your Giving and People Portfolio

A T THIS POINT, you're probably thinking about two questions. First, *How much should I give?* And second, *How do I know whom to give to?*

Giving will require revising your current budget to make room for investing in the people and causes you care about. If you're living on 100 percent of what you make, you're skating on thin ice. There is no margin for emergencies or the unexpected. In addition, living month-to-month doesn't give you the flexibility to serve others. Consider cutting unnecessary expenses, like subscription services you rarely use, downsizing, renting out a room in your house, getting a second job, or discussing the guidelines for a pay raise with your boss.

We've said this before, but it bears repeating: a life well lived is not determined by your bank account but by how you *spend* your bank account. Ramit Sethi says, "A rich life is lived outside the spreadsheet."[1] What's more, "If we can start giving earlier in life, whether it's five dollars or fifty thousand dollars, that is a critical part of a rich life."[2] You can earn more, save more, and give more—all at the same time.

The following giving strategies are great starting points:

Model 1: 80-10-10. Live on 80 percent, save 10 percent, give 10 percent.

If you're on a pretty strong financial footing—you have consistent income, not a lot of debt, and your spending is under control—Model 1 is for you. Now take 10 percent of your income and start giving it away according to your Generosity Purpose.

Model 2: 70-10-10-10. Live on 70 percent, save 10 percent, pay down debt 10 percent, give 10 percent.

If you have debt you are paying off, Model 2 is great for you. Refer to the debt-reducing strategies listed in Part 1. You want to build up your savings to three to six months of committed living expenses, and then reevaluate your budget. Model 2 requires you to reduce your spending in order to begin saving and giving.

Model 3: the variable option. Start giving 1 percent of your income and then decide how much to save and aggressively pay down your debt. Reduce your spending according to the strategies mentioned in Part 1. You'll likely never miss the 1 percent you are giving, and the psychological rewards are well worth it. Then increase your giving fund by at least 1 percent per year as you knock your debt down and increase your savings.

Kara and I followed Model 2 as struggling newlyweds who still wanted to make giving to our church and other organizations a priority. As our income increased, we transitioned to Model 1 and have made it our goal to increase our giving every year. We got the idea from a couple at our church just after we were first married. They told us they started by tithing 10 percent of their income, but every year they increased it just slightly. Kara and I have tried to follow their model, increasing our giving each year even if it's in small increments: 10.1 percent, 10.2 percent, 10.5 percent.

The ultimate giving budget? Aim to live on 10 percent and give away the rest. Let me simplify it for you again in four simple steps:

1. Give 1 percent now.
2. Increase your giving percentage each year.
3. Make giving 10 percent your goal.
4. Aim toward living on 10 percent and giving away the rest.

This week, sit down with your favorite drink, turn on some classical music, and begin to make changes to your current budget. Pick the model that works best for you and your family and write a plan for how to stick with it. Then gather your family around the table, pick your Generosity Purpose, and start giving together.

Now it's time to put your money into motion. Let's talk about how.

I know you want to be a good steward of your money and make good choices when it comes to diversifying your investment portfolio. Equally important is to diversify your giving strategy. When it comes to giving, many consider it a one-trick pony. "If I give to the Salvation Army, I can't give to the local homeless shelter." "If I give to the animal rescue down the street, I can't give to Meals on Wheels." "If I give to my church, that's enough." No, it's not—diversify!

Look beyond the obvious. Look around you and you'll see individuals in your life in need—friends, family, strangers. They might not be hungry or homeless, but with a little boost from you, they can know you believe in them to achieve their dreams.

I call this group of people my "People Portfolio." Of course, your portfolio will include your own family. Every year I start a family meeting by asking my wife and each of my kids to set goals for the coming year and to reflect on their progress with their goals during the past year. I then ask each of them: "What can Mom and I do to help you reach what is most important to you?" Over the years the answers have ranged from sports lessons, camps, and exercise equipment, to getting evaluated to identify their career and personality strengths. I'm careful not to live my dreams through them or insist that they follow my path. I want them to have the tools that help extract every ounce of potential they have, when they're ready.

But what about other people who could use some help and encouragement? A friend you could treat to dinner once in a while; another friend who doesn't have the $600 to fix their car's brakes; an acquaintance with a great idea but without the knowledge, experience, or wherewithal to capitalize on it.

There's a secret art to giving that is really fun: anonymous giving. Kara and I are big believers in it. We get such pleasure from dropping money in a mailbox or sending someone an anonymous check. Just remember to disguise your handwriting by writing with your weak hand.

I'll give you an example. A family friend was visiting one day, and she began talking about a CD she wanted to record and market to youth camps. During the course of our conversation, she mentioned she was trying to save the large sum of money it would take to get her project off the ground. The following weekend I got my family together and we hatched a plan. I went to the bank and had them draw up a cashier's check for the amount she needed. My daughter then put it in an envelope and left it in her mailbox. The next time we saw her, she told us she had received an anonymous check that had paid for her to record the CD. She was nearly jumping up and down with enthusiasm and had no idea it was us who had left the gift. We weren't about to tell her.

I have many memories of one of my children quickly hopping out of our car, slipping an envelope underneath a doormat, ringing the doorbell, then sprinting back to the car so we could drive away before anyone came to the door. This is a super easy and fun way to give with your kids.

Sometimes giving isn't in the form of a cashier's check, or any money at all. Non-monetary gifts can give someone a similar boost, even if it's just a weekly text of encouragement. If you see value and promise in a person, think about how you can help that person make their mark in the world.

So many people say, "I have this dream. I want to write a book or release this song. I want to create a business or do something that's been brewing in my head for years, but I don't have the resources to do it." You can be their dream funder, and believe me, it feels as good for you as it does for them. You'll get your best dividends by investing in people. It makes you a better person *and* a better investor. And of course, we now know that it also makes you happier, healthier, and wealthier!

There's a list of names in my phone of people I text every week. Among them are each of my kids, some of their friends, and students who attend the Business Club I teach. Each name is special to me because I know they have the potential to do great things. Every week, I send out a short text of encouragement to each name on that list.

I want to provide opportunities for young people that nobody gave me. If you could go back to your younger self, what would have encouraged you to fulfill your potential? That's what you now have a chance to do. It could be the young person you know who is bright but needs a break. Maybe they don't have the money to start junior college. The spectrum of giving is endless, from Tom Golisano building a children's hospital, to paying for someone's coffee behind you in the drive-thru. Here are some of my personal favorites:

- Keep homeless packs (with items like blankets, socks, bottled water, and peanut butter jars) in the back of your car to give away at every opportunity.
- Give a cashier's check or cash anonymously to someone in need.
- Perform a monthly audit of what you have around the house that you never use and donate the items to your local charity-run resale shop.
- Have some fun on the investment side by saying to yourself, "I'm going to put a small amount of money into this stock, and if it does really well, I'll donate the profit to my favorite charity." (By the way, that means you'll pay no capital gains taxes on it!)
- Fund a family member's or friend's first year of community college.
- Pay for a course or certification that will aid a family member or friend in an area that interests them.
- Sponsor a child through an organization like World Vision or Compassion International.
- Anonymously send a newly married couple gift cards for groceries or a fun date night.

The options are limitless. Together with your spouse and family, choose your giving strategy, define your People Portfolio, and select a few action steps to start implementing. Put your money in motion now.

CHAPTER 34

What Really Matters

A FEW YEARS ago I drove up to Waco to visit my daughter Lauren, who was a sophomore at Baylor University. As we ate pancakes and eggs in a sticky vinyl booth at IHOP, she shared what a hard time she was having and the anxiety she was facing both about her schoolwork and the social scene. As we finished our meal and the waiter brought our check, we decided to do something fun and leave a large tip. Lauren and I snuck out of the restaurant and back to my car and watched through the window as the waitress picked up the check from our table. Her reaction was priceless, and so was the time laughing and giggling with my daughter as we blessed someone else.

I believe teaching your children to give with a generous heart is one of the best things you can do as a parent. I'll let you in on a little secret: You don't need a lot of money to start giving. You can start small, and you can start early.

Charity begins at home. When people, even if they have very minimal means, ask, "How can I help make someone else's life better?" an entire shift of thinking occurs. It may sound very small, but it's actually very, very big. Whether it's $1, $5, or $20, you're saying, "I'm taking my hard-earned money and I'm giving it to somebody else." It changes how you think about money. You are the giver of a blessing to someone else.

Other families are realizing how much this outlook on life can impact their kids and the world. John O'Leary explained to me that his business is primarily as a motivational speaker, so when the COVID-19 pandemic hit, more than 90 percent of his top-line revenue disappeared nearly overnight. There was one particular day when he was struggling, licking his wounds, and feeling sorry for himself. But he remembers that even in the midst of hardship, he wanted to show his kids what leadership looks like. "You're not just called to be joyful when you're on top of the world. You're called to be joyful when you feel like you're beat down by it."[1]

John told me he was determined to set the right example. As a family, they agreed they'd make changes in their spending habits and in the way they stayed generous. That's how he put it: how they would *stay* generous. "Boys, watch Dad. Watch. We're gonna stay generous."[2]

Then in May, just a couple of months after the virus hit the United States, John learned he was going to receive a sizable royalty check for his book *In Awe: Rediscover Your Childlike Wonder to Unleash Inspiration, Meaning, and Joy*, which had just landed on several bestseller lists.

"I wanted to show my kids God's desire in our hearts to be generous in all seasons—*all* seasons—so we had a conversation around the dinner table [about how to divvy up the royalty check]," John explained. "The decision was made . . . that we were gonna give it all away, 100 percent of the proceeds were gonna go to Big Brothers Big Sisters," which is an organization the whole family supports.[3]

John said that once their decision had been revealed, other corporate sponsors recognized what his small business was doing and said to themselves, "'Well, gosh, if they can do that, maybe we can do likewise.' So there have been five other corporations that have come alongside us and have also written checks to Big Brothers Big Sisters. Good begets good."[4]

While emphasizing the importance of giving, John said newspaper headlines have given him a reason to continue discussing things that really matter with his children. "We talk about some of the injustices. We've been talking about this recession. We're talking about their own dad who had his revenue cut . . . dramatically because I wanted my kids on the inside—not so they get scared, but so they recognized this is real."[5]

Does your family need a reset? Is it time to sit down together and say, "You know what? We want to be a giving family. We're going to set aside $10, $25, $50, or $100 a month. We're going to have a family meeting together and each month, we'll be asking ourselves, 'How can we use this money to bless someone?'"

Connect the theoretical to the practical. Ask your kids to keep an eye out for any needs they see. Maybe the parent of a classmate lost their job. Ask your child, "What do you think that means to their family? How do you think they are paying for their house, car, or gas? What do you think it means to your friend in terms of their ability to go with you to the movie or eat out at a fast-food restaurant?" Together, brainstorm some ways to help. Perhaps there is an organization that does a lot to help people in your community that needs extra items, like blankets, during the cold season. Imagine with your kids how it would feel to have to try to sleep without a blanket. Ask if they would be willing to give one of their blankets so someone else can sleep warmly. See, now you've begun to foster a mindset of giving.

The impact we have on people. The good we do in the world. This is what really matters.

CHAPTER 35

Give at Work

ONE OF MY favorite things about giving is that you can do it in so many different ways—and it doesn't always involve breaking out your checkbook.

In addition to advising clients how to save and where to invest, part of my job was to show them how to establish a procedure for giving. Sometimes it's not the kind of giving they expected, particularly if they're doing all they can to keep up with their own monthly bills. It's a simple idea, yet many have never considered it before: give at work.

I often hear from friends and clients who feel frustrated that their job is devoted exclusively to making money. They want more out of their job, more out of their life. You might feel the same way—and I've got good news. Within almost any job, there are opportunities for doing good.

"Job purposing" is what Bea Boccalandro calls this principle. She told me several stories that illustrate the point particularly well. In one, an inner-city parking attendant walks around his place of work and systematically measures every car's tires. If someone's tires are bald, he tells the owner or puts a note on the dash. He leaves at the end of his workday feeling like he's made a difference and made it less likely that someone would have a flat tire or blow out on their way home.[1]

Another story Bea told me is a great example of the kind of work that inspired her to write her book, *Do Good at Work*, in the first place.[2] After a speech she gave in Seattle, a woman came up to her who was an administrative assistant at a regional trucking company. Her colleagues had nicknamed her "TP Tina." Tina had been working late one evening when she noticed the janitorial staff throwing away partially used rolls of toilet paper and replacing them with new ones. That may have made sense to avoid the calamity of some unfortunate soul running out of paper in the middle of the workday, but tossing half- or three-quarter-used rolls was tremendously wasteful. So Tina asked the janitorial staff to drop them off at her desk. Soon her office was covered with rolls of toilet paper. Now, a few times a week, Tina delivers the toilet paper to a local homeless shelter, which has saved enough money on its grocery bill to be able to host a monthly ice cream social for the families living there.[3]

The world could use more stories like Tina's. Companies often take the lead for you, in which case joining their pro bono or charitable initiatives is often the easiest way to start feeling good about your job. Many companies encourage their employees to get involved in the same causes they're promoting at the corporate level, often by asking for donations from employees during a certain time of year. Some companies will offer opportunities to volunteer at charitable organizations during the workday—with pay.

You don't have to rely on your company to lead the way to doing good in the workplace. Take your cue from TP Tina and think out of the box. Or in the box. Sometimes a way to do good sounds obvious only in retrospect. It can be as simple as where you decide to make a reservation for your team's corporate luncheon. If you settle on a restaurant that helps local farmers or one that hires at-risk youth or special needs adults, now you've shifted an ordinary task to one that makes a difference.

Over the past decade, several hotel chains have started having their housekeeping staff collect partially used soap and shampoo bottles. These items are then donated to a nonprofit, like Clean the World Foundation, which sterilizes them and then provides hygiene to poverty-stricken communities around the world.[4] This is transforming what would be waste into a valuable benefit for people in need, and it has a positive impact on the morale of the housekeeping staff.

Recently a manager at a chemical manufacturing plant, where safety is a big concern, announced that every day the team didn't have a safety violation, the company would donate ten dollars to a local nonprofit that benefits their community. This company has more than one hundred plants around the world, and the strategy to reward safety with charity has spread to other large companies.[5]

Bea Boccalandro makes the point that it is possible for anyone to go home proud of their work by answering one question: "How can I do one or more of my tasks in a way that is more charitable, equitable, environmentally sustainable, or otherwise more purposed?"[6] She adds that it might take a few weeks, but we eventually come up with a practical answer because, "We're hardwired to make a contribution. It's against our nature not to."[7]

There are as many ways to give back at your job as there are jobs. Be creative. Whatever you're doing to earn a living—working full-time, in your home or out of it, whether you're feeling confident in making ends meet or if you're barely making it, there's something you can do to introduce your version of good into the world. And that's a feeling that builds momentum. No longer is all your energy focused on your job and just getting by.

Now you're working with a sense of purpose, of meaning, which will make you work harder, better, faster.

Don't keep mailing it in from nine-to-five. Work with a purpose.

CHAPTER 36

Eternal Investing

I WAS AT the gym recently and someone shared with me that their dear friend had just passed away. "Derrick," he said to me, "you never know when your last day on earth is going to be. Make sure you leave it all on the table."

His comment made a deep impression on me. It reminded me of a simple illustration done by Randy Alcorn, author of *The Treasure Principle*. It's so simple yet so profound.

You can see that it's just a dot, followed by a bold line, with an arrow at the end of the line:

The dot represents the short time we have on earth, and the line with an arrow represents eternity.[1] In that dot is everything that happens to you during your lifetime—births, graduations, weddings, funerals, jobs, kids, grandkids, vacations—the highs and lows of your life. We get so caught up in the dot that we lose sight of the idea of eternity. Like it says in James 4:14, "You are a mist that appears for a little while and then vanishes."

Think about the dot not as just those fleeting eight or nine decades of your existence. The purpose of the dot is to lay the foundation for what comes next, for eternity. Tomorrow is not promised to any of us, so what we do now is what counts. That's what my friend meant by "leaving it all on the table."

"Let's face it, at the end of our lives, we're not gonna count how much money we have," says Jon Gordon. "It's not gonna matter what kind of car we drove, what kind of house we have. When we die, it's gonna matter: Did we make a difference in the lives of others? Did we make an impact? Did we leave a legacy?"[2]

Until you've taken your very last breath, you can still have the powerful impact you're looking for.

John O'Leary told me about a favorite poem of his called "The Bridge Builder" by Will Allen Dromgoole.[3] It's the story of a man, near the very end of his life, who builds a bridge across a vast, fast-moving river. A presumably much younger man on the other side of the river calls to him and asks why the old man is bothering to build a bridge when he will never come this way again. The old man responds that he is not building the bridge for himself; he's building it for the younger men who will come behind him.[4]

That's the question to ask yourself. Not *what* you are going to do today or tomorrow, but *how* it will have an impact long after you're gone. In the movie *Gladiator*, Russell Crowe plays a Roman general, Maximus. As he and his men are about to attack, he says to them, "Hold the line, stay with me!" And then he says something powerful: "Brothers, what we do in life echoes in eternity."[5]

Now, you're probably thinking, "How does focusing on the line rather than the dot relate to giving?" It has everything to do with it. I call it investing in the *eternal economy*.

In Economics 101, the future value of money is always greater than its present value.

Why? Because you can invest it now and make more money. One dollar placed in virtually any reasonable investment vehicle will be worth more ten, twenty, or thirty years into the future. Logically, therefore, the time value of money means that by investing money today and allowing it to grow means a larger amount in the future, so you should give it away upon your death.

In the eternal economy it's just the opposite. The present value of money is worth more than the future value. Why? Today's impact value is greater. Hear me out.

Upon their death, most people leave their greatest gifts to their children, their children's children, and maybe other family members. Often they will also include bequests to organizations they have supported during their lifetime. This strategy is admirable, but it locks up your money so it can't be used for good today. The beneficiaries have to wait ten, twenty, thirty, or more years before the money will have any kind of impact. Consider this: what would happen if you decided to concentrate your giving on the here and now? Even if you give a smaller amount today, it unlocks the ability for that money to immediately begin impacting people's lives. If you provide money to improve a school system, your contribution toward giving children a better education will have an exponential impact. Those kids are going to grow up and have families of their own and be productive, some no doubt because of you. It's like a farmer saying, "I'm going to wait a couple years to plant these seeds because they'll improve in the package." No. The seeds get better once they're in the ground and can start to grow. Your giving today is adding value to lives, and that value is projected forward into eternity.

Here's a specific example. Let's say you decide to leave a bequest in your will for $10,000 to Doctors Without Borders. Well, that's great. I'm sure the organization will welcome that $10,000. The problem is, the $10,000 may go to them in ten years, twenty years, thirty years from now. But what if you gave them a smaller amount today, say, $2,000? That money can change the lives of people today and will surely have a multiplier effect because those people who were saved by that $2,000 will have had decades of leading productive lives, probably with children of their own who have also, even if indirectly, benefited from your gift.

Sit down with your spouse, your family, your investment advisor, and implement the giving strategy that you've put in place. Money put in motion creates waves. Remember, your money can either be a stagnant pond of water that doesn't move at all or a river where value continues to flow.

By diligently and consistently giving now and not later, you can flip a person's paradigm. I see this across all demographics—people making more money so they can give more, giving more so they can earn more. It's a beautiful cycle. It's the eternal economy, the cycle of giving that keeps paying dividends forever. That's something you cannot achieve with any other investment.

CHAPTER 37

The Good Money Challenge

JANUARY 15, 2020.

That's the date I sold my financial planning business after twenty-five years. I came to that day after quite a bit of prayer, many discussions with my wife, and a lot of reflective thought. Most of the thinking had to do with what I wanted the next twenty-five years of my life to look like, and I came to the conclusion that I wanted to pursue my passion of teaching others to earn more, save more, and give more so they can live a life of purpose. I realized my vision would require selling my business and launching something new. I knew it would not be without struggle, not unlike many of you out there trying new jobs or adventures. But if you've ever had a dream, put your mind to it, and fought with determination while wondering if it was going to work, I know that feeling. But somewhere along the way you start to enjoy the journey and it begins to feel worth the huge leap of faith. Your purpose fuels your progress.

Good Money Revolution is not just motivational—it's purposeful. Motivation can come and go, but if you have a purpose, you'll fight, you'll sacrifice, you'll do whatever it takes to climb the hill. The key is to *connect your cash to a cause, your money to a movement, your profits to a purpose.*

The old way of thinking about money is over. Today you've been handed a reset button, and we know successful people press that button frequently.

Today you're looking forward. No more looking backward; enough is enough. It's time to revolt against your old ways of thinking about money and those mindsets you may have formed when you were barely past childhood and have thoughtlessly repeated. Done. Kaput. Finished.

You are now a *giver*. Life isn't about you anymore. It's bigger than you. This is about making a conscious decision to make your life stand for something, to make a difference, to make the world a better place—all through your Generosity Purpose.

Picture your ideal life: playing with your kids or grandkids, traveling to tropical beaches, building relationships with new friends, and working hard at your job to give profits away to the causes you care deeply about. Picture the impact you could have.

If you don't, here's what's at stake: impact will be lost, people's lives will be left unchanged, and you will remain unfulfilled with your money and your life.

The way you're choosing to use your money can change your family, your health, your wealth, your happiness, your fulfillment, and the world. It's time to believe it. So I end by asking you to take the Good Money Challenge.

Good Money Challenge

- I believe that money is good. Good money in the hands of good people gets good work done.

- I choose to give my money strategically to make the world a better place through my Generosity Purpose.

- I accept the Good Money Challenge to earn more, save more, and give more.

The Good Money Revolution starts now.
Are you ready?

Signature: _____

Date: _____

Download the Good Money Challenge at
www.GoodMoneyFramework.com/Challenge

Connect with Derrick

Derrick's passion is helping you grow your net worth so you can use it for good.

EMAIL: Derrick would enjoy hearing from you by email at derrick@goodmoneyframework.com.

SPEAKING: Derrick is available to inspire and engage your audience, organization, or team. If you're interested in having Derrick speak at your event, go to goodmoneyframework.com/keynote.

PODCAST: Listen to the top-rated *Good Money* podcast where you'll get practical money and business advice, learn why it pays to be generous, and see why money is not bad and you should have more of it. Subscribe now wherever you listen to podcasts.

For more easy and practical tips on making and managing your money, join the Good Money Community.

  @derricktkinney

  facebook.com/derrickkinneyFB

  linkedin.com/in/derrickkinney

Acknowledgments

I T'S A POWERFUL force when people believe in you. My sincere appreciation goes out to each of these rock stars who helped launch *Good Money Revolution* into the world.

Kara, my better half in this fun adventure, thank you for your unwavering belief in me. I'm glad you pushed me to jump in and write this.

Lauren, your writing expertise and leadership guided this important work to completion. Thank you for always asking, "How can we help improve each reader's life?"

Don Miller, I'll never forget sitting across the table from you on that May morning. You helped breathe life into this big idea of mine and here we are. You'll never know the depth of my gratitude and respect for you as a thought leader and trusted friend. The Good Money Revolution has begun. It's time to remake the world.

John O'Leary, my first *Good Money* podcast guest. When someone is the first to bet on you, it's not forgotten.

Adam Grant, my words are inadequate to express how helpful you've been. I'm grateful for your impact on so many lives, including mine.

Adam Snyder, thank you for helping me mold my ideas and concepts into a practical message that will change lives.

Lastly, so much appreciation for Hector Carosso and my team at Skyhorse Publishing. Thank you for believing the world needs this message.

Notes

Chapter 2

1. Laura Sapranaviciute-Zabazlajeva et al., "Link Between Healthy Lifestyle and Psychological Well-Being in Lithuanian Adults Aged 45–72: A Cross-Sectional Study," *BMJ Open* 7, no. 4 (April 2017): https://www.doi.org/10.1136/bmjopen-2016-014240.

2. James J. Lachard (Jim Brown), "An Interview with God," quoted in Martin Fox, "'An Interview with God'—I Stand Corrected...," Center for Global Leadership, June 30, 2012, https://centerforgloballeadership.wordpress.com/2012/06/30/an-interview-with-god-i-stand-corrected/.

3. Dr. Richard J. Tunney, *The Effects of Winning the Lottery on Happiness, Life Satisfaction, and Mood*, September 2006, 2, https://worlddatabaseofhappiness-archive.eur.nl/hap_bib/freetexts/tunney_rj_2006.pdf.

4. Andrew T. Jebb et al., "Happiness, Income Satiation and Turning Points Around the World," *Natural Human Behavior* 2 (January 2018): https://doi.org/10.1038/s41562-017-0277-0.

5. Daniel Kahneman and Angus Deaton, "High Income Improves Evaluation of Life but Not Emotional Well-Being," *Proceedings of the National Academy of Sciences* 107, no. 38 (August 2010): https://www.princeton.edu/~deaton/downloads/deaton_kahneman_high_income_improves_evaluation_August2010.pdf.

Chapter 3

1. Ed Diener et al., "The Satisfaction with Life Scale," *Journal of Personality Assessment* 49, no. 1 (1985): https://doi.org/10.1207/s15327752jpa4901_13.

2. Scott Hankins, Mark Hoekstra, and Paige Marta Skiba, "The Ticket to Easy Street? The Financial Consequences of Winning the Lottery," *Review of Economics and Statistics* 93, no. 3 (August 2011): https://doi.org/10.1162/REST_a_00114.

3. Hankins, Hoekstra, and Skiba.

4. "Research Statistic on Financial Windfalls and Bankruptcy," NEFE, January 12, 2018, https://www.nefe.org/news/2018/01/research-statistic-on -financial-windfalls-and-bankruptcy.aspx.

5. Erik Lindqvist, Robert Östling, and David Cesarini, "Long-Run Effects of Lottery Wealth on Psychological Well-Being," *Review of Economic Studies* 86, no. 6 (November 2020): https://doi.org/10.1093/restud/rdaa006.

6. John O'Leary, "Invest in Others for Lasting Wealth," interview by Derrick Kinney, October 19, 2020, in *Good Money*, podcast, MP3 audio, 28:25, https://open.spotify.com/episode/0q52Qr1acYWjYcjBfOBavt?si=6c5639b 46beb436c.

Chapter 4

1. Elizabeth W. Dunn, Lara B. Aknin, and Michael I. Norton, "Spending Money on Others Promotes Happiness," *Science* 319, no. 5870 (March 2008): https://www.doi.org/10.1126/science.1150952.

2. Michael Norton, "Money Can Buy You Happiness," interview by Derrick Kinney, November 23, 2020, in *Good Money*, podcast, MP3 audio, 17:25, https://open.spotify.com/episode/5fvubbhrngRy6MUH0TnC9W?si=s7X M7uioQkGTg9pKQlUB-g&dl_branch=1.

3. Anne Frank, "Give!," in *Anne Frank's Tales from the Secret Annex*, ed. Gerrold van der Stroom and Susan Massotty (London: Halban Publishers Ltd., 2010), 85.

4. O'Leary, "Invest in Others for Lasting Wealth," 15:19.

5. Norton, "Money Can Buy You Happiness," 2:35.

6. Jon Gordon, "From Average to Greatness: How to Create True Wealth and Significance," interview by Derrick Kinney, September 29, 2020, in *Good Money*, podcast, MP3 audio, 28:25, https://open.spotify.com/episode/6ag5g 7g2TMSgTBEncdjHOb?si=ykyYCDHjR3e5h1Q0dE4WCw&dl_branch=1.

Chapter 5

1. Rabbi Daniel Lapin, "Why the Pursuit of Money Is Not Bad," interview by Derrick Kinney, November 2, 2020, in *Good Money*, podcast, MP3 audio, 44:30, https://open.spotify.com/episode/4rJvY9JzkhPz2jGE8o9laV?si=Bk20Xo 2dQ6muceymGCkp2g&dl_branch=1.

Chapter 6

1. Bea Boccalandro, "How Doing Good at Work Can Make You More Money and Reduce Stress," interview by Derrick Kinney, September 24, 2020, in *Good Money*, podcast, MP3 audio, 17:35, https://open.spotify.com/episode /2eAevEKkmbACgzL91Ksyd2?si=5YOsfSBcQvCALhUIkr_WSw&dl_ branch=1.

2. Boccalandro, 18:19.

3. Boccalandro, 19:22.

4. Boccalandro, 20:17.

5. "Giving Back," Bombas, accessed October 6, 2021, https://bombas.com/pages/giving-back.

6. Boccalandro, "How Doing Good at Work Can Make You More Money and Reduce Stress," 15:56.

7. Boccalandro.

8. Drew and Ellie Holcomb, "How Challenging Times Provide the Greatest Opportunities," interview by Derrick Kinney, October 1, 2020, in *Good Money*, podcast, MP3 audio, 25:49, https://open.spotify.com/episode/7vSdHyB2MhWhLwoa0nKFVo?si=a8dGXMVYSgu0xkovfgFu1g&dl_branch=1.

9. Holcomb, 24:40.

10. Holcomb, 25:15.

Chapter 7

1. Stephen King, *Rita Hayworth and Shawshank Redemption* (1982; repr., New York: Scribner, 2020), 110.

2. "He Has Achieved Success Who Has Lived Well, Laughed Often and Loved Much," Quote Investigator, June 26, 2012, https://quoteinvestigator.com/2012/06/26/define-success/#more-4036.

3. Brian Buffini, Turning Point 2011, Dallas event.

4. Michael Gerber, "3 Secrets to Be Your Own Boss," interview by Derrick Kinney, November 5, 2020, in *Good Money*, podcast, MP3 audio, 26:53, https://open.spotify.com/episode/1hNL3ZsbYDe90h1zkAywKs?si=5_r865PgSVi1JfooYLti9Q&dl_branch=1.

Chapter 8

1. Morgan Housel (@morganhousel), Twitter, August 3, 2020, 4:27 p.m., https://twitter.com/morganhousel/status/1290383765907226624?lang=en.

2. Morgan Housel, "How to Make More Money Than Most People," interview by Derrick Kinney, December 28, 2020, in *Good Money*, podcast, MP3, 2:39, https://open.spotify.com/episode/5FzMnitHilKpHFa3NnOGGn?si=r550-5gYSLi2As41kyVEqQ&dl_branch=1.

Chapter 9

1. Bola Sokunbi, "Ditch Debt and Build Real Wealth," interview by Derrick Kinney, February 8, 2021, in *Good Money*, podcast, MP3, 4:47, https://open.spotify.com/episode/3EjVFfNk8kOyws0MCljw1r?si=WJfj_WZhQBuLmzSOqASTPg&dl_branch=1.

2. Sokunbi, 6:17.

3. Sokunbi, 7:07.

4. Sokunbi, 2:23.

5. Sokunbi, 3:05.

6. Lara Casey, "Take a Risk for What Really Matters," interview by Derrick Kinney, October 22, 2020, in *Good Money*, podcast, MP3, 11:10, https://open.spotify.com/episode/1plZYnsvPVRmviDxao5hfh?si=IficI3pbSK-q2x9pAQAEYA&dl_branch=1.

Chapter 11

1. Michael Hyatt, "How to Get More Done by Doing Less," interview by Derrick Kinney, October 5, 2020, in *Good Money*, podcast, MP3, 3:47, https://open.spotify.com/episode/2Wy6TH80SBvQeLStEKGmy8?si=6G8r126oSLyJ0bYl9LyIEQ&dl_branch=1.

2. Ryan Pineda, "How to Flip Your Way to Real Estate Millions," interview by Derrick Kinney, June 14, 2021, in *Good Money*, podcast, MP3, 30:10, https://open.spotify.com/episode/12m0ySWz4akEFMqwhn4iIR?si=ah2XZoJHSWWgo5ghwjjCkg&dl_branch=1.

Chapter 12

1. The average player salary in Major League Baseball was $4.17 million in 2021, according to the Associated Press. The top players make much more than that, of course. At the beginning of the 2021 season, shortstop Francisco Lindor signed a $341 million ten-year contract with the NY Mets. Associated Press, "Average MLB Salary at $4.17 Million, Down 4.8% from 2019," ESPN, April 16, 2021, https://www.espn.com/mlb/story/_/id/31270164/average-mlb-salary-417-million-48-2019.

2. Ramit Sethi, "Spending Less Is the Wrong Strategy," interview by Derrick Kinney, January 18, 2021, in *Good Money*, podcast, MP3, 11:23, https://open.spotify.com/episode/0mG5WfjJweShDqKeKXSCF8?si=fvIfeOh1RqK-ZgRNHcUfIQ&dl_branch=1.

3. Sethi, 13:17.

4. Sethi, 13:38.

5. Sethi, 14:20.

6. Sethi, 14:33.

7. Sethi, 15:25.

8. Sethi, 15:45.

9. Dan Miller, "How to Love Mondays & Find Your Purpose," interview by Derrick Kinney, November 16, 2020, in *Good Money*, podcast, MP3, 30:39, https://open.spotify.com/episode/4q6EwQs9q6Nxw8kyEIazta?si=Gy4d5msXRkumAArAWibGJw&dl_branch=1.

10. Miller, 31:50.

Chapter 13

1. Chris Myers, "Burning the Boats: How We Found Success By Getting Rid of Our Safety Net," *Forbes*, June 8, 2016, https://www.forbes.com/sites/chrismyers/2016/06/08/burning-the-boats-how-we-found-success-by-getting-rid-of-our-safety-net/?sh=1af0e72a2371.

2. Hyatt, "How to Get More Done by Doing Less," 23:44.

3. William Goldman, *Adventures in the Screen Trade: A Personal View of Hollywood and Screenwriting* (1983; repr., New York: Warner Books, 1984), 39.

4. Marc Randolph, "Turn Everyday Problems into Extraordinary Profits," interview by Derrick Kinney, January 4, 2021, in *Good Money*, podcast, MP3, 44:31, https://open.spotify.com/episode/1fUuu59EhMu3ywr1IXbOJK?si=lQ375U6gRHyocF1mdWtDfg&dl_branch=1.

5. Randolph, 43:36.

6. Casey, "Take a Risk for What Really Matters," 12:05.

7. Dan Miller, "How to Love Mondays & Find Your Purpose," 2:39.

Chapter 14

1. *The Shawshank Redemption*, directed by Frank Darabont, staring Morgan Freeman (Beverly Hills, CA: Castle Rock Entertainment, 1994), DV, 2:17:12.

2. Matthew McConaughey, "Who Said Money Is Bad?," interview by Derrick Kinney, January 11, 2021, in *Good Money*, podcast, MP3, 5:28, https://open.spotify.com/episode/5fLquF5MPyuLe7VJbbojZs?si=n4BcNzwuReqpV47yaqMfbw&dl_branch=1.

3. McConaughey, 7:07.

4. McConaughey, 10:49.

5. Gordon, "From Average to Greatness," 26:05.

Chapter 15

1. Jay Samit, "The Faster You Fail, the Faster You'll Succeed," *Wall Street Journal*, April 16, 2015, https://www.wsj.com/articles/BL-232B-3571.

2. Tom Golisano, "Billionaire Secrets to Grow Your Business," interview by Derrick Kinney, December 21, 2020, in *Good Money*, podcast, MP3, 5:03, https://open.spotify.com/episode/3CFdxuAcba11Xe2acZWdpb?si=fL6gNizhQjqDitTfcBgviw&dl_branch=1.

3. Jesse Cole, "Change the Rules So You Win Big," interview by Derrick Kinney, October 15, 2020, in *Good Money*, podcast, MP3, 16:27, https://open.spotify.com/episode/7IsGgYWAv2auBrTBVnU2TK?si=5C07y5T1Q1SoxXan_wP5iw&dl_branch=1.

4. Casey, "Take a Risk for What Really Matters," 18:05.

5. Hyatt, "How to Get More Done by Doing Less," 24:45.

6. Marshall Goldsmith, *Mojo: How to Get It, How to Keep It, How to Get It Back If You Lose It* (New York: Hyperion, 2009), 10–12.

Chapter 16

1. Gordon, "From Average to Greatness," 22:23.

2. Andy Andrews, "The Missing Ingredient for Your Next Big Decision," interview by Derrick Kinney, November 30, 2020, in *Good Money*, podcast, MP3, 13:59, https://open.spotify.com/episode/6sj7O5ptvt8iWg5wpDWzyX?si=B beXg-MsQ-OznOyJnIZ_zQ&dl_branch=1.

3. Theodore Roosevelt, "Citizenship in a Republic" (Sorbonne, Paris, France, April 23, 1910), American Presidency Project, University of California Santa Barbara, https://www.presidency.ucsb.edu/documents/address-the-sor bonne-paris-france-citizenship-republic.

Chapter 17

1. "USS Huron Historic Shipwreck Preserve," North Carolina Office of State Archaeology, accessed October 7, 2021, https://archaeology.ncdcr.gov/uab/heritage-dive-sites/huron.

Chapter 18

1. Richard Fry, "Millennials Overtake Baby Boomers as America's Largest Generation," Pew Research Center, April 28, 2020, https://www.pewresearch.org/fact-tank/2020/04/28/millennials-overtake-baby-boomers-as-americas-largest-generation/.

2. "Boomer Expectations for Retirement 2019: Ninth Annual Update on the Retirement Preparedness of the Boomer Generation," Insured Retirement Institute, April 2019, https://www.myirionline.org/docs/default-source/default-document-library/iri_babyboomers_whitepaper_2019_final.pdf?sfvrsn=0.

Chapter 20

1. Sokunbi, "Ditch Debt and Build Real Wealth," 9:26.

2. Lapin, "Why the Pursuit of Money Is Not Bad," 1:57.

3. Lapin, 13:33.

4. "Jeff Bezos," Bloomberg Billionaires Index, accessed October 7, 2021, https://www.bloomberg.com/billionaires/profiles/jeffrey-p-bezos/?sref=p7z S9UoY.

5. https://www.cnbc.com/2019/05/16/how-jeff-bezos-dad-who-came-from-cuba-alone-at-16-inspires-him.html.

6. Laurel Wamsley, "MacKenzie Scott Is Giving Away Another $2.7 Billion to 286 Organizations," NPR, June 15, 2021, https://www.npr.org/2021/06/15/1006829212/mackenzie-scott-is-giving-away-another-2-7-billion-to-286-organizations.

7. Golisano, "Billionaire Secrets to Grow Your Business," 16:02.

8. O'Leary, "Invest in Others for Lasting Wealth," 8:09.

Chapter 21

1. "The National Study of Millionaires," Ramsey Solutions, September 27, 2021, https://www.ramseysolutions.com/retirement/the-national-study -of-millionaires-research.

Chapter 22

1. The term "Money Scripts®" was coined by financial psychologist Brad Klontz in a 2011 study where he found that people have four basic attitudes toward money: money avoidance, money worship, money status, and money vigilance. We do not intend to take credit for his ideas or usage of the term and want to give credit where credit is due.

Chapter 23

1. Sethi, "Spending Less Is the Wrong Strategy," 34:01.
2. Sethi, 29:02.
3. Donald Miller, *Scary Close: Dropping the Act and Finding True Intimacy* (Nashville, TN: Thomas Nelson, 2014), 127.
4. Jon Acuff, "Stop Overthinking and Start Living," interview by Derrick Kinney, April 12, 2021, in *Good Money*, podcast, MP3, 12:00, https:// open.spotify.com/episode/3HPybleppkByrb4CMN2rih?si=GGUB-feqRSZG4aNZ3NpFa4g&dl_branch=1.

Chapter 24

1. Kelsa Dickey, "Budget Isn't a Bad Word," interview by Derrick Kinney, December 14, 2020, in *Good Money*, podcast, MP3, 28:45, https://open .spotify.com/episode/3qMTJEaL62sqpziGtOltcV?si=nokpnJXoSni3A9lb_ S8YoQ&dl_branch=1.

Chapter 26

1. Dickey, 23:34.
2. Sokunbi, "Ditch Debt and Build Real Wealth," 11:05.
3. Dickey, "Budget Isn't a Bad Word," 19:552.
4. Dickey, 20:54.

Chapter 28

1. Lizzie Likness, "Community Rallies for Homeless College Student Living in a Tent," CNN, July 18, 2016, https://www.cnn.com/2016/07/17/us/ iyw-fred-barley-homeless-college-student-bikes-six-miles/index.html.
2. Cathy Free, "A Teen Buys Repossessed Storage Units at Auction, Then Gives the Contents Back to the Original Owners," *Washington Post*, June 16,

2021, https://www.washingtonpost.com/lifestyle/2021/06/14/storage-unit-auction-teen-owner/.

Chapter 29

1. Kent Youngstrom, "Profit from the Power of Surprise," interview by Derrick Kinney, October 8, 2020, in *Good Money*, podcast, MP3, 23:18, https://open.spotify.com/episode/2Smv2CyZmAiSpQyTpJsMdm?si=BIQpii IwTHGSbmdkoGG8-w&dl_branch=1.

2. James H. Fowler and Nicholas A. Christakis, "Cooperative Behavior Cascades in Human Social Networks," *Proceedings of the National Academy of Sciences of the United States of America* 107, no. 12 (March 2010): https://doi.org/10.1073/pnas.0913149107.

3. Cole, "Change the Rules So You Can Win Big," 30:37.

4. Norton, "Money Can Buy You Happiness," 6:25.

5. Lara B. Aknin et al., "Prosocial Spending and Well-Being: Cross-Cultural Evidence for a Psychological Universal" (working paper, National Bureau of Economic Research, Cambridge, MA, September 2010), http://doi.org/10.3386/w16415.

6. Vicki Contie, "Brain Imaging Reveals Joys of Giving," National Institutes of Health, June 22, 2007, https://www.nih.gov/news-events/nih-research-matters/brain-imaging-reveals-joys-giving.

Chapter 30

1. Paul Zak, Angela Stanton, and Sheila Ahmadi, "Oxytocin Increases Generosity in Humans," *PLOS ONE* (November 2007): https://journals.plos.org/plosone/article?id=10.1371/journal.pone.0001128.

2. Stephen Post, *Why Good Things Happen to Good People: How to Live a Longer, Healthier, Happier Life By the Simple Act of Giving* (New York: Broadway Books, 2007), 48.

3. Doug Oman, Carl E. Thoresen, and Kay Mcmahon, "Volunteerism and Mortality Among the Community-Dwelling Elderly," *Journal of Health Psychology* 4, no. 3 (May 1999): https://doi.org/10.1177/135910539900400301.

4. Stephanie L. Brown et al., "Providing Social Support May Be More Beneficial Than Receiving It: Results from a Prospective Study of Mortality," *Association for Psychological Science* 14, no. 4 (July 2003): https://doi.org/10.1111/1467-9280.14461.

5. Rachel L. Piferi and Kathleen A. Lawler, "Social Support and Ambulatory Blood Pressure: An Examination of Both Receiving and Giving," *International Journal of Psychophysiology* 62, no. 2 (November 2006): https://doi.org/10.1016/j.ijpsycho.2006.06.002.

6. Angela Thoreson, "Helping People, Changing Lives: 3 Health Benefits of Volunteering," Mayo Clinic Health System, September 16, 2021,

https://www.mayoclinichealthsystem.org/hometown-health/speaking-of
-health/3-health-benefits-of-volunteering.

Chapter 31

1. Jason Feifer, "Giving Back Is Good Business," interview with Derrick Kinney, January 25, 2021, in *Good Money*, podcast, MP3, 2:42, https://open .spotify.com/episode/5ByuObQSmnJzuV44A00HQc?si=sEKW1TSq TM-fmcUU343q_g&dl_branch=1.

2. Feifer, 6:41.

3. Blake Mycoskie, "How I Did It: The TOMS Story," *Entrepreneur*, September 20, 2011, https://www.entrepreneur.com/article/220350.

4. Mycoskie, "How I Did It: The TOMS Story."

5. Boccalandro.

6. K. Eriksson et al., "Generosity Pays: Selfish People Have Fewer Children and Earn Less Money," *Journal of Personality and Social Psychology* 118, no. 3 (2020): https://doi.org/10.1037/pspp0000213.

7. Charles Antis, "Give More to Grow More (Why Every Nail Matters)," interview by Derrick Kinney, October 29, 2020, in *Good Money*, podcast, MP3, 11:18, https://open.spotify.com/episode/4cLn6xaZJ7aOpgYWXLYL 4H?si=3T4zzSlVRYuKT9jm9399pg&dl_branch=1.

8. Ken Rusk, "Be a Millionaire (No College Required!)," interview by Derrick Kinney, October 26, 2020, in *Good Money*, podcast, MP3, 30:50, https://open.spotify.com/episode/0tE5ABJyVanH2LP3eEKQ17?si=_20B fAzmR-W5t6x689HVwg&dl_branch=1.

9. Rusk, 31:17.

Chapter 32

1. Matthew 19:16–26, my paraphrase.

2. Steven Pressfield, "This One Thing Is Keeping You From Making Money," interview by Derrick Kinney, May 3, 2021, in *Good Money*, podcast, MP3, 2:22, 4:30, https://open.spotify.com/episode/3jY5NUUgNN9kf4Rf 4GAwDe?si=vNH5NqwgQwOG_DYIbsVL9A&dl_branch=1.

Chapter 33

1. Sethi, "Spending Less Is the Wrong Strategy," 39:41.

2. Sethi, 46:55.

Chapter 34

1. O'Leary "Invest in Others for Lasting Wealth," 9:05.

2. O'Leary, 9:49.

3. O'Leary, 10:08.

4. O'Leary, 11:43.

5. O'Leary, 13:55.

Chapter 35

1. Boccalandro, "How Doing Good at Work Can Make You More Money and Reduce Stress," 37:42.

2. Boccalandro, 3:10.

3. Boccalandro, *Do Good at Work: How Simple Acts of Social Purpose Drive Success and Wellbeing* (New York: Morgan James Publishing, 2021), 66.

4. "Hospitality Program," Clean the World, accessed October 6, 2021, https://cleantheworld.org/get-involved/hotel-recycling-program/.

5. Boccalandro, "How Doing Good at Work Can Make You More Money and Reduce Stress," 38:25

6. Boccalandro, 36:40.

7. Boccalandro, 32:30.

Chapter 36

1. Randy Alcorn, *The Treasure Principle: Unlocking the Secret of Joyful Giving*, rev. ed. (New York: Multnomah, 2017), 52.

2. Gordon, "From Average to Greatness," 8:38.

3. O'Leary, "Invest in Others for Lasting Wealth," 7:34.

4. Will Allen Dromgoole, "The Bridge Builder," Poetry Foundation, accessed October 4, 2021, https://www.poetryfoundation.org/poems/52702/the-bridge-builder.

5. *Gladiator*, directed by Ridley Scott, featuring Russell Crowe (Hollywood: Universal Pictures, 2000), DV, 6:46.